THE NATIVE STORIES FROM
KEEPERSofLIFE

Walking at Night in the Desert

Flowers of the cactuses
faded and dry,
flames which burned
at the tips of green arms,
light the darkness with memory.

As I walk
I ask the stones
older than any
I have known before
to let me pass this way in peace,
to go as the bird
goes through the air,
leaving little changed.

I speak to the sage plant
as I gather it,
May I pick you, my friend?
And when it agrees
I feel it lift itself
from the soil to my hand.

—Joseph Bruchac

THE NATIVE STORIES FROM
KEEPERS OF LIFE

Told by *Joseph Bruchac*

Michael J. Caduto and Joseph Bruchac
Foreword by Marilou Awiakta
Story illustrations by
John Kahionhes Fadden and David Kanietakeron Fadden

FIFTH
HOUSE
PUBLISHERS

Canadian Cataloguing-in-Publication Data
Caduto, Michael J.
     The Native stories from Keepers of life
Canadian ed. —
ISBN 1-895618-62-2
1. Indians of North America - Folklore - Juvenile
literature.   I. Bruchac, Joseph, 1942–
II. Caduto, Michael J.   Keepers of Life.   III. Title.

E98.F6C33 1995   j398.2'089'97   C94-920274-6

Printed in the United States of America
99 98 97 96 95 / 5 4 3 2 1

Editor's note: In the introduction, this book is referred to as *Native Plant Stories*,
which is its American title. Apart from the title and minor differences in the front
matter, the Canadian and American editions of this book are otherwise identical
in every respect.

Fifth House Ltd.
620 Duchess Street
Saskatoon, SK, Canada
S7K 0R1

This book is dedicated to Chan Kin and Robert Bruce,
to Gladys Tantaquidgeon and Barre Toelken
and to all those Elders who have helped me remember
that we humans must care for and respect all that grows.

Contents

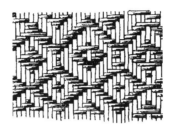

Foreword

A bridge is a gift to the people. A life line.

Living near the mighty Mississippi River, I'm constantly thankful for our two bridges. An old maxim says, "We see what we are taught to perceive." My father taught me to appreciate the skill of bridge builders, emphasizing that they must work in harmony with the laws of nature. So when I look at the two bridges I see that their long spans are well grounded in both banks and their lengths are held in balance by supports below and above. Because they are strong yet flexible, the bridges hold fast in the elements. They were built with respect. They are beautiful. They are reliable.

It is the same with the books of the *Keepers* series. Using the ancient wisdom of Native North American stories as the connecting span, Michael J. Caduto and Joseph Bruchac have respectfully built bridges of understanding between people and the natural world—first in *Keepers of the Earth*, then in *Keepers of the Animals* and *Keepers of the Night*. Now comes *Keepers of Life* and *Native Plant Stories*, which unify humans, plants and all that lives in the great cycle of coming and going, giving and receiving that is life itself. As the authors say, "Plants stand between all life on Earth and eternity." Because of this scope, the balances in the book are necessarily complex and intricate.

Chief among them is the authors' very careful choice of stories. As I began the book I thought, "How are they going to choose? The distance to be spanned is so great, not only between plants and people, but also between cultural perceptions." When I finished reading, I realized that Caduto and Bruchac had chosen the stories by working in harmony with the laws that Nature taught Native North Americans to perceive millennia ago: *Everything in the universe is related in one family. All life is equal. Generative power is gender-balanced—male and female. And to keep life going, all these relationships must be kept in balance.* These are Original Instructions, laws instilled in Nature by the Creator. In presenting the stories, Caduto and Bruchac faithfully adhered to the laws and to the language Native peoples use to express them, a language which is gendered and familial—Mother Earth, Father Sky and so on. For fun, and also to have a visual pattern, I marked the stories with male and female symbols. Clearly, the authors have preserved the healthful traditional balance, where both genders are equally vigorous Keepers of Life. I saw what I have been taught to perceive—an inclusiveness that begins in the very heart of the universe and extends to "all our relations."

Corn—*Zea mays*—exemplifies this concept and has upheld it to Native peoples for seven thousand years. In his beautiful and extraordinary cover illustration for *Keepers of Life*, John Kahionhes Fadden has rendered what they perceived in the plant. From the union of male tassel and female silks comes the nutritious ear, whose seeds continue the generations. And so it is with humans. In their creation story, the Mayans say that the Creator and the Maker made human beings from cornmeal, from maize. In the stories of all Native peoples, the spirit of the plant teaches the wisdom of respect; sometimes the spirit is female, sometimes male. Appropriately, Fadden has portrayed the spirit in a form that could be either gender and holds in the outstretched hand an unmistakable message: balance.

The span of stories is well grounded in knowledge of science and human cultures. All along its length, it is supported by supplemental text and activities. Readers—adults and children alike—will understand how all life is interconnected in one continuous cycle and requires respectful care. However, teaching students to perceive the balance and mutual respect of genders may need special emphasis because, comparatively speaking, contemporary society is just beginning to teach perception of female presence and roles. From a Native North American perspective, what are women doing in the stories?

Women continue the generative power of Mother Earth, renewing, nourishing and sustaining the life of the people. Traditionally with food, men have been the hunters and women have been the principal caretakers of plants, which comprise 80 percent of human food. Women, as well as men, act decisively to preserve life.

In the Huron creation story, "The Sky Tree," the people lived in the Sky Land where a great tree furnished all their food. The old chief was sick. In a dream he saw that fruit from the top of the great tree would cure him. He told his wife Aataentsic, "Ancient Woman," to cut down the tree and bring him the fruit. At the first stroke of her axe, the tree split and fell through a hole in the sky. Aataentsic told her husband what had happened, then said these very important words: *Without the tree, there can be no life. I must follow it.*

Looking up from the waters below, Turtle saw Aataentsic falling. Like a clan mother, she organized help, telling the other animals to bring up soil from beneath the waters and pile it on her back. "Aataentsic settled down gently on the new Earth and the pieces of the great tree fell beside her and took root."

Immediately following this story is "How Kishelemukong (the Great Mystery) Made the People and the Seasons." He caused the first men and the first women to sprout from the branches of an ash tree. Then he created the four directions and the seasons that would come from these directions. The West, North and East were Grandfathers, governing the times of Fall, Winter and Spring. South was a Grandmother, bringing the warmth and new life of Summer. To make sure the divisions among the seasons were fair and acceptable, Kishelemukong decided to have Grandfather North and Grandmother South play a hand game that would hold the seasons in balance. "And so it is to this day."

And so the balance continues in the stories.

Like men, women teach the law of respect to the people—and sometimes have to relearn the law themselves. In an Inuit story, Nunam-shua, "the Woman Who Dwells in the Earth," punished a disrespectful hunter. To a hunter whom she had observed to be respectful, Nunam-shua gave the gift of success. In "The First Basket," the mother cedar gave some of her slender roots to a woman and showed her how to make a basket. The basket was Cedar's daughter. When the woman sang her thanks, the basket walked beside her and carried her load. Another woman was not so wise. She didn't sing thanks to her basket, and was greedy besides. The basket refused to walk. "And from that time on, no basket ever again carried a load on its own for the people."

Women teach children their first lessons in survival and well-being. They also gage the cycles of life and ceremony. The story of how Waynabozho brought wild rice to the people begins with his grandmother calling him to her lodge. "'Grandson,' Nokomis said, 'it is time for you to go to some distant place in the forest and fast. Then a dream may come to you to help the people yet to come.'" She helped him plant the first rice seeds he found, then sent him out again to learn the further good he needed to know. Thus the generations cooperate in bringing a new food for the people.

As *Native Plant Stories* circles toward completion, the Osage story of "The Buffalo Bull and the Cedar Tree" brings a vision of healing for the people and "all our relations." At the beginning of the story a man from the Peace Clan uses an arrow flecked with feathers stained red from pokeberry juice to bring peace to Buffalo Bull. Healing plants grow where Buffalo rolls on the ground. He gives the people different kinds of corn and squash to eat and, finally, Buffalo offers himself as food, shelter, clothing and tools. The people then find the cedar. She stands in the midst of the four winds, sending forth her fragrance. "'I stand here on this cliff,' Cedar said, 'so that the Little Ones may make of me their medicine.'" And she shows the people her gnarled roots and bending branches with their feathery white tips as symbols of long life. Cedar becomes medicine, a symbol of longevity to the people and is their Tree of Life. Because Buffalo Bull and Cedar give openly of themselves, the Osage people ultimately discover ways to live well. And they continually express their thanks to the Creator for these gifts.

The stories teach us to perceive our relatives in the universe as bridges from the Creator, life lines that sustain us in body and spirit. Our relatives are beautiful. They are reliable. And if we keep them with respect, maintaining the balance of giving and receiving, they will hold us in balance so that we, in turn, can help heal Mother Earth and our people. This is the message and the hope of *Native Plant Stories*. It is a gift to the people. And to the "seeds of the people"—our children.

—Marilou Awiakta

Listening to the Plants

I stood on the porch of a cabin next to Paradox Lake in the Adirondack Mountains of northern New York. My friend, Swift Eagle, a Pueblo/Apache elder from the southwest, stood next to me. As I leaned over the railing, looking far out over the lake, I noticed that Swift Eagle was standing very quietly, his face close to the branches of an ash tree that hung over the porch.

"What are you doing?" I said.

"Listening," he said, a small smile on his face.

"What are you listening to?" I asked.

"I'm listening to the leaves."

Although that happened many years ago, I've never forgotten the lesson it taught me. We are often so busy scanning the horizon, looking for big things coming from far away, that we fail to notice those things that are closest to us. We do not notice the grass—or the flowers—beneath our feet; we do not listen to the songs of the leaves. We take for granted the rooted, growing plants that are all around us, and we fail to recognize or remember that all life on this planet depends upon them.

Native traditions, and the stories in this book, do not take the plants for granted. They are life and we, as human beings, owe our continued existence on this earth to the plants. In the European way of thinking, plants are objectified. A plant may be useful, decorative or a weed. Plants are unaware, without feelings and meant to be manipulated—cut like a lawn or a tree, harvested like the fruits and vegetables in our orchards and gardens or labeled as nuisances and rooted out. In the Native way of thinking, though, the plant people are as aware and as deserving of respect as are those living beings that do not have roots—such as humans.

It goes further, however, than just our attitude toward the plants. In Native traditions, the plants interact with human beings on a more active basis. Just as, in Native stories, human people and animal people are able to communicate freely with each other and even walk in each other's worlds, so too the plants are able to speak with human beings and enter their lives in a variety of ways. The traditions of the Haudenosaunee people offer us one example. Among the Haudenosaunee, the six allied Native nations most often known as the Iroquois, the three principal plants in their gardens are Corn, Bean and Squash. They are called The Three Sisters and (in Seneca) *Diohe'ko*, "These Sustain Us." The three are often pictured as lovely maidens, as close as sisters, and, as any student of agricultural science could tell you, they are plants that grow very well in association with each other. The bean needs to climb and the corn stalk is a natural trellis. The squash spreads out over the ground beneath the corn and shades out other plants that might choke the roots of the corn. Furthermore, each of the three plants takes different nutrients from the soil. There are numerous ceremonies related to the planting and harvesting of The Three Sisters, and certain songs are to be sung during these times of planting and harvest. In the Seneca Green Corn Ceremony, which takes place around the month of August, the leader of the ceremony speaks directly to the Corn saying *Diettinon'nio diohe'kon*, which means "We give thanks to you who sustain us." It is believed that these ceremonies and songs will make the plants feel happy and appreciated, and, in turn, the plants will grow better and produce a larger harvest for the people.

Where did these ceremonies and songs come from? In most cases, Haudenosaunee traditions explain that the songs and ceremonies were taught to the people by the plants. In some cases, they came to someone long ago in a dream or a vision, in which, for example, the Corn took the shape of a person and spoke directly to the person, telling him or her what to do. In other cases, someone might be walking in a corn field and hear a song being

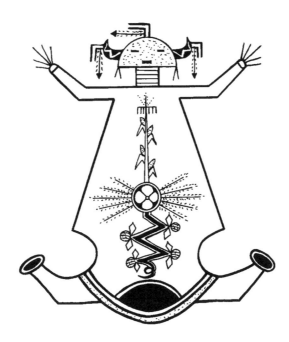

sung when no other human was around. Hearing such a song, one could only conclude that it was being sung by the plants themselves and given as a gift to the people.

More so than in the modern western world, the Native relation between plants and people is seen as a balance. The plants give us those things we need—food, shelter, clothing and even the air we breathe—but we must give back to them in return. We may give such tangible things to the plants as water and nutrients or, just as important in the Native view, we may give them verbal thanks in the form of words that are spoken or sung. The plants are aware of such gifts. The whole concept of the awareness of plants is a relatively new idea to European thought, but a very old truth among the Native nations of the Americas. I have heard it said again and again by Native herbalists, people who use the leaves and seeds and roots and bark of various plants for healing, that the way a certain plant can be used was taught to them or their elders by that plant itself. The Cherokee tradition about healing plants tells us that diseases, such as rheumatism, were sent to human beings by the animals to punish the humans for their mistreatment of the animals through overhunting or forgetting to give thanks to the animals. Being compassionate beings, however, the plants took pity on the humans and offered themselves as medicines to cure those sicknesses.

It is also commonly said among Native healers that you cannot go out to gather medicine plants unless you have good thoughts in your mind. If your thoughts are bad or confused, "the plants will hide from you." Sweetgrass and sage, aromatic plants that are said to promote good health through their healing scent, are two such plants that seem to make themselves hard to find, even in areas where they grow in abundance. An Abenaki friend of mine whose late father, Mdawelasis, was one of my own teachers, went one day to gather sweetgrass in a place where her father had told her she could find it. She was in a hurry that day and grew more and more frustrated looking for the sweetgrass and not finding it. Finally, she gave up in disgust, concluding that the sweetgrass no longer grew there. Some months later, her mother went with her to that same spot. My friend parked her car just where she had parked it before and climbed out to help her mother look. Her mother, however, was already gathering sweet-grass, which was growing there by the roadside right next to the car.

Not only do Native stories tell us that the plants are able to communicate with us and may be our teachers, they also say that the plants are our relatives in the most literal sense. There are many traditions throughout the world that explain where human beings came from. The two dominant stories in European traditions are the biblical tale of creation in which God created Adam (whose name *Adham* means "Earth" in Hebrew) from the soil and the Darwinian tale of creation in which human beings evolved from ape-like beings. In more than one Native tradition, the people come from neither earth nor animals. The Abenaki tale says that human beings were created from the ash trees after the human beings made of stone proved to be too hard-hearted and heavy-footed. The Lenape tale in this book tells how people sprang from a great tree. In a similar way, the Mayan story, "The People of Maize," tells how humans were made from the corn.

Of course, one does not have to take these stories literally to learn from them. Native traditions are filled with metaphor, and teaching through a story means learning not just the story itself, but hearing and seeing the lessons that the story helps us internalize. Today, more than ever, we need stories that help us sustain life. Without such stories to guide us, terrible things can happen. I have only to think of the trip I took some years ago to visit the Lacandon Maya people in the Chiapas province of Mexico. Only fifty years ago, that province was green and moist with jungle, teeming with thousands of varieties of birds and insects, animals and plants. Lacandon Maya traditions teach that we must respect the jungle and the trees and not cut them down indiscriminately. But, as we drove for mile after mile along the dry, dusty road, I saw few trees. The jungle, which had been taken from the control of the Lacandon people, had been clear-cut for its lumber and made into pastures for cattle. Yet those cattle pastures would produce grass only for a few years before finally losing the few nutrients they had left after the rainforest was cut down. Within a few years, where there was once a vast self-sustaining ecosystem, there would be a desert which would support almost no life at all. The European tradition of using the forest and land to make money in the short term was producing ecological and human disaster in the long term. Suddenly, I saw green ahead of us—the edge of the lands still under ownership of the Lacandon Maya. As we went up a hill and rounded a corner, we found ourselves in the shade of a canopy of great trees. All around, for the first time that day, I heard the voice of the forest—the sounds of wind in the leaves, the songs of birds and insects. Then, only a hundred yards into that small jungle, the rain began to fall.

One of the oldest teachings among Native people is that we must always turn back to the natural world for guidance. Everything in the world was given original instructions by our Creator on how to be. That is true of the stones, the plants, the waters, the animals, the winds—all things. Humans, too, were given original instructions. Of all the living things in creation, however, only the humans are prone to forget those instructions. Fortunately for us, the natural world remembers and is ready to teach us. The plants are among our best teachers. These stories of the plants and the sources of life, taken from Native nations as different from each other as the Inuit of the Arctic north and the Maya of the highland jungles of Central America, are wonderful examples of the lessons we can learn. To begin to learn, all that we need to do, as my friend Swift Eagle has taught me, is to listen.

—Joseph Bruchac

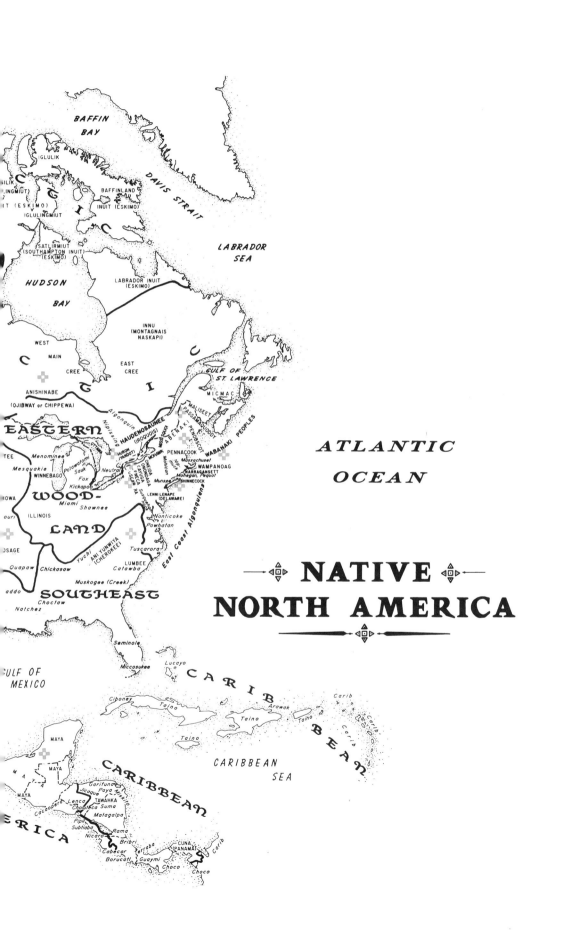

BAFFIN
BAY

DAVIS STRAIT

IGLULIK
(INGMIUT)

ARCTIC

BAFFINLAND
INUIT (ESKIMO)

IT (ESKIMO)

IGLULINGMIUT

LABRADOR
SEA

(SATLIRMIUT
(SOUTHAMPTON INUIT)
(ESKIMO)

ARCTIC

HUDSON

BAY

LABRADOR INUIT
(ESKIMO)

INNU
(MONTAGNAIS
NASKAPI)

WEST

MAIN

CREE

EAST
CREE

SUBARCTIC

GULF OF
ST. LAWRENCE

ANISHINABE

(OJIBWAY or CHIPPEWA)

MICMAC

Algonquin

Nipissing

MALISEET

PASSAMAQUODDY

EASTERN

HAUDENOSAUNEE
(IROQUOIS)

WABANAKI PEOPLES

PENOBSCOT

ABENAKI

TEE

Menominee

Potawatomi

HURON
(WYANDOT)

MOHAWK

PENNACOOK

Mesquakie

Sauk

ONEIDA

Mohican

Massachuset

WAMPANOAG

WINNEBAGO

Fox

Neutral

ONONDAGA

CAYUGA

NARRAGANSETT

Kickapoo

Erie

SENECA

Nanticoke

Mohegan, Pequot

IOWA

WOOD-

Miami

Shawnee

Munsee

SHINNECOCK

ILLINOIS

LENNI LENAPE
(DELAWARE)

our

LAND

OSAGE

Wanticoke

Powhatan

Quapaw

Chickasaw

Yuchi

ANI YUNWIYA
(CHEROKEE)

Tuscarora

addo

Natchez

SOUTHEAST

Choctaw

Muskogee (Creek)

LUMBEE

Catawba

East Coast Algonquians

ATLANTIC

OCEAN

→ ◈ NATIVE ◈ →
NORTH AMERICA

Seminole

Miccosukee

Lucayo

CARIB

GULF OF
MEXICO

Ciboney

Taino

Carib

Arawak

Taino

Taino

Carib

Carib

BEAN

Taino

CARIBBEAN
SEA

MAYA

CARIBBEAN

MAYA

M A Y A

Garifuna

Paya Miskito

Jicaque

MAYA

Lenca

TAWAHKA

Cacopera

Choluteca

Suma

Cacaopera

Subtiaba

Matagalpa

Pipil

ERICA

Nicarao

Rama

Bribri

Cabecar

Terraba

CUNA
(PANAMA)

Guaymi

Carib

Borucatl

Choco

Choco

NATIVE
PLANT STORIES

Introduction

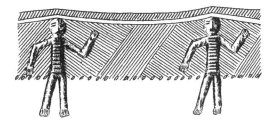

*An old man
dressed in torn
clothing sat
weeping.*

The Corn Spirit

Long ago, they say, there was a village of people whose cornfields were blessed with good harvests, year after year. They had so much corn each year that they began to take it for granted. They stopped weeding the fields and the children trampled the cornstalks as they played. When harvest time came, the people picked, but they did not do it well. Much of the corn was left unpicked and only the birds ate it. The people wasted more than they ate. They threw ears of corn to their dogs. As they had always done, they dried some of the corn to eat in the winter and use for seed corn the next spring. They placed this corn in storage baskets to bury for the winter, but they did everything carelessly. The corn baskets were not well made. The storage holes were not dug deeply or well covered.

"There is much game in the forest," the people said. "We can always hunt to survive, even if the stored corn spoils."

So the people went on without showing respect for the corn that gave them life. They even forgot to say thanks to the Creator for their good fortune.

Only one man remembered to show respect. His name was Dayohagwenda. Dayohagwenda cared for his fields and weeded them. He harvested his corn carefully and gave thanks for his good harvest. He stored his corn with great care. He was sad about the way the others acted.

That autumn, after the harvest moon, the people went hunting. But the hunters had bad luck. Animals were hard to find. It seemed that the deer and moose and even the rabbits had all disappeared from the forest. The people tried to fish, but the streams and lakes were empty. Finally, the people dug up their stored corn. But the poorly made baskets had fallen apart. Much of the corn had been eaten by mice. The rest had rotted away.

"What shall we do?" the people said. "We will starve."

Meanwhile, Dayohagwenda was walking in the forest. He was thinking about the way his people no longer showed respect for the corn or gave thanks. As he walked, he found an old trail. It led to a clearing in the forest. In that clearing was a lodge made of elm bark and built on top of a mound of earth. Weeds grew all around the lodge. In front of the lodge, an old man dressed in torn clothing sat weeping.

"Grandfather," Dayohagwenda said, "why are you weeping?"

"I am weeping because your people have forgotten me."

"Why are your clothes torn?"

"They are torn because your people threw me to their dogs."

"Why are you so dirty?"

"I am dirty because your people let their children trample me."

"Why are there weeds around your lodge?"

"Your people no longer take care of me. Now I must go away and I can never return again to help them."

Now Dayohagwenda knew who the old man was. He was Corn Spirit.

"Grandfather," Dayohagwenda said, "do not leave us. I still respect you. I will go back and remind my people how to treat you."

The old man stopped weeping. "Grandson," he said, "I will stay with *you*. If your people show me respect, I will not leave them."

Dayohagwenda went back to the village.

"We are going to starve," the people said. "Our corn is gone and we have no other food."

"Listen," said Dayohagwenda, "I have been in the forest. There I found a lodge surrounded by weeds and an

old man wearing torn clothing the color of cornhusks. He said his people deserted him and he was going to leave forever."

The people understood. "It is Corn Spirit," they said. "He has left us and now we will surely die."

"No," said Dayohagwenda, "I spoke with Corn Spirit. I told him we would treat him with respect. He said that if we respect him, he will help us through the winter."

Then Dayohagwenda dug up his own stored corn. His baskets had been well made. He had dug his granary deep and covered it properly. All of his harvest was there. There was more than he had remembered storing, much more. There was enough to feed the whole village through the winter. There was even enough left to use as seed corn for planting in the spring when the leaves of the maple tree were the size of a squirrel's ear.

From then on, Dayohagwenda's people always showed respect for the corn. They planted with care and hoed and weeded. They sang songs of thanksgiving as they harvested. They made strong baskets and deep storage pits for their granaries. Most of all, they remembered to give thanks for the blessing of corn and all of the other good things they had been given. They taught their children and their children's children to do the same. So it is to this day.

They planted with care and hoed and weeded.

Creation

Aataentsic took
her husband's
stone ax
and went to
the great tree.

KAHIONHES

The Sky Tree

In the beginning, Earth was covered with water. In Sky Land, there were people living as they do now on Earth. In the middle of that land was the great Sky Tree. All of the food which the people in that Sky Land ate came from the great tree.

The old chief of that land lived with his wife, whose name was Aataentsic, meaning "Ancient Woman," in their longhouse near the great tree. It came to be that the old chief became sick and nothing could cure him. He grew weaker and weaker until it seemed he would die. Then a dream came to him and he called Aataentsic to him.

"I have dreamed," he said, "and in my dream I saw how I can be healed. I must be given the fruit which grows at the very top of Sky Tree. You must cut it down and bring that fruit to me."

Aataentsic took her husband's stone ax and went to the great tree. As soon as she struck it, it split in half and top-pled over. As it fell a hole opened in Sky Land and the tree fell through the hole. Aataentsic returned to the place where the old chief waited.

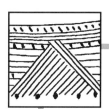

"My husband," she said, "when I cut the tree it split in half and then fell through a great hole. Without the tree, there can be no life. I must follow it."

Then, leaving her husband she went back to the hole in Sky Land and threw herself after the great tree.

As Aataentsic fell, Turtle looked up and saw her. Immediately Turtle called together all the water animals and told them what she had seen.

"What should be done?" Turtle said.

Beaver answered her. "You are the one who saw this happen. Tell us what to do."

"All of you must dive down," Turtle said. "Bring up soil from the bottom, and place it on my back."

Immediately all of the water animals began to dive down and bring up soil. Beaver, Mink, Muskrat and Otter each brought up pawfuls of wet soil and placed the soil on the Turtle's back until they had made an island of great size. When they were through, Aataentsic settled down gently on the new Earth and the pieces of the great tree fell beside her and took root.

"Bring up soil from the bottom, and place it on my back."

How Kishelemukong Made the People and the Seasons

L ong ago, Kishelemukong, the Great Mystery, built the world. First Kishelemukong caused a great turtle to rise up from the depths of the water and float on the surface. Then Kishelemukong took moist earth and placed it on the back of the giant turtle as the turtle floated in the endless ocean. The ridges of Turtle's back turned into mountains, and grass and shrubs and trees of all kinds began to grow from the soil.

It went on this way for some time, but Kishelemukong felt that something was yet to be made. There were birds and animals and living things of all kinds, but there was something yet to be made. Kishelemukong considered shaping beings from the stones of Earth. But such beings would be heavy-footed and they would crush the plants beneath them.

Instead, Kishelemukong made a straight ash tree grow up tall. From its branches the first men and the first women sprouted.

Then Kishelemukong placed the sun in the day sky and the moon in the night sky. And so that all would grow and

Sometimes one
of them has
better luck than
the other.

rest in its proper time, Kishelemukong created the four directions and the seasons which would come from each of those directions. West and North and East were Grandfathers, governing the times of Fall and Winter and Spring. South was a Grandmother, bringing the warmth and new life of Summer. Like the trees and the plants, human beings grew to love that time of the year and their Grandmother South the best of all.

Then Kishelemukong decided to make sure the divisions between the seasons were fair and acceptable.

"It will be this way," Kishelemukong said. "Each year there will be a contest between Grandfather North and Grandmother South. They will play the hand game. One will take a bead and hide it in one hand or the other so that the opponent must guess which hand it is held in. Each will have 12 sticks and each time a winning guess is made, one stick will be taken. Whenever Grandmother South begins to win more sticks, the weather will begin to turn warm and Spring will come. But when her luck begins to change, Autumn will be a signal that Grandfather North is winning his sticks back again."

And so it is to this day. Because the game between Grandmother South and Grandfather North is so evenly matched, the seasons are always about the same length, but as in every game, sometimes one of them has better luck than the other and so we never know for sure when each season will end or begin.

Celebration, Thanksgiving and Stewardship

"That tree
standing there,
the Maple,
it is a
special tree."

The Thanks to the Trees

(This comes from the traditional Seneca Thanksgiving Address, adapted and translated from a Long Opening Thanksgiving Address given in 1972 by Enos Williams/Quivering Leaves at Seneca Longhouse, Six Nations, Ontario.)

A nd now we will speak again.

Our Creator decided trees will be on Earth, growing here and there; also forests will be growing of trees, groves will be growing on Earth. And it is still true that trees grow here and there. Our Creator decided this will be something important, for from these trees medicines can come. And certain it is, they are still growing, all of them are different in the way they grow.

Our Creator decided all of the trees will have names, every one of them that people will know them, the people who will live here on Earth. And it is possible that from those trees, within their families, people will grow well. It is possible that people will draw on those trees when it changes, the wind, when it grows colder, the wind. It is possible that then people will be kept warm and they will work together as one, kept warm by that which he left, the live coals on Earth.

Our Creator decided the trees will work together well to bring happiness to families on Earth. And we still think it is

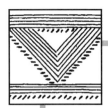

coming to pass in this manner. And carefully now, the Creator decided, "The trees will have this one to lead them. People living on Earth will say, 'That tree standing there, the Maple, it is a special tree.'"

Our Creator decided "When it becomes warm, the wind, it is then that the sap will flow, so it is that the maple trees will be tapped, from there it will be collected that it may be boiled down by the people. And so then it will be possible for the people to drink the maple syrup again."

And it is possible then that people will be gathered; it is important also that people gather together then. Medicine will be made from the maple syrup, and people moving about, people on Earth will be helped. And when it became warm, the wind, it is true that we saw again this new sap was rising. And it came to pass that we drank the maple syrup again. And it was possible that we were gathered together at what we call Maple Sugar Gathering, the Maple Festival.

And so it is we thank our Creator in the way that he left it we should always thank him at ceremonies. And we think this ceremony has come to pass. Let us put together our thoughts that we will always be grateful, for it is certain that he is sending them to us, the trees which are standing on Earth. We are the ones our Creator thought of; those trees were meant to be used well by those of us moving about on Earth.

Carefully now, it is that we thank him, the one who dwells in the sky, Sonkwaiatison.

"The trees will have this one to lead them."

Flowers and Fruits, Seeds and Spores

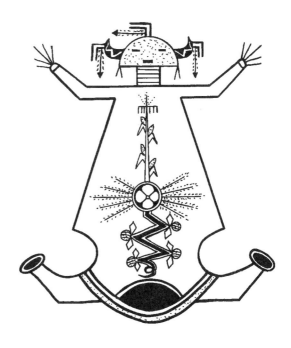

*Then he said
good-bye to the
People of
First Light.*

The Circle of Life and the Clambake

Everything in life is a circle. Everything is alive—the animals, the birds, the plants of Earth and the plants of the seas, the water, the air and the stones—and everything must be respected. All things are part of Earth, which gives us everything we need. When we take from Earth, we must give back in return. The Medicine Circle is the source of our strength.

So the Wampanoag people explain the way they have been instructed by the Creator. For untold centuries, the Wampanoag, the People of First Light, have lived along the southeastern coast of Massachusetts. And their traditions and stories relate to that circle of life which human beings must strive to maintain.

One of the heroes of the Wampanoag is a giant whose name is Maushop. Some say he lived there on the narrow land now called Cape Cod even before the Wampanoags arrived. He was not alone, for there were other beings there with him. One of his friends was a giant frog which was his closest companion.

Maushop's life was a good one. He swam in the waters of Popponesset Bay. He made great fires on the sandy beach

to cook whales and other sea creatures, and when he emptied the sand into the sea from his great moccasins he made the islands of Nantucket and Martha's Vineyard.

The Wampanoag became the friends of Maushop and he enjoyed helping them. When they wanted to cook or keep themselves warm, he would carry great loads of wood on his back for their fires. When they were hungry he would drive whales onto the shore so that the people did not have to hunt for food. He was so good to the people that they became lazy.

Then Kehtean, the Great Spirit, spoke to Maushop.

"It is good that you care for your younger brothers," Kehtean said, "but it is not right that you do everything for them. They are like little children when you care for all their needs. They must take responsibility for their own lives or they will never grow. If they do not care for themselves, how can they care for the rest of Creation? Their circle will not be strong."

"It is true," Maushop said. Then he said good-bye to the People of First Light. His small friends watched him from the cliffs at Gay Head as he waded into the bay, which was greenish brown with rockweed, and swam away toward the west. As he swam, Kehtean, the Creator, transformed him into a great white whale. Maushop's friend, the giant frog, came to the cliffs, filled with sorrow at the loss of his friend. Kehtean took pity on the giant frog and changed him into a huge stone, which still sits there at Gay Head, looking out to

"They must take responsibility for their own lives or they will never grow."

sea. That stone reminds the Wampanoag that Kehtean cares for all things and that the decisions of the Great Mystery are made for the good of all.

Without their friend to help them, the Wampanoag wondered how they would survive. They soon found, however, that when they worked for themselves, everything that they needed was there. One of those ways of survival which makes use of all that is around them—Earth, the plants, the animals and the water—is called by them *Appanaug.* It is a word which means "seafood cooking," and, because it is a special part of the circle, it is done to honor someone or to mark the change of the seasons.

With thanks in their hearts and with care, they wade into the shallow waters of Popponesset Bay and collect some of the Rock People, old round stones which have been smoothed by the tide. They find a place in the forest which feels right, and there they make a circle and dig a shallow, round hole in the earth. The stones are then placed in that hole, and the shape of the stone and the shape of that hole remind the Wampanoag of the Medicine Circle of all life.

Dry wood is gathered from the forest. No living trees are used. That way they clear the forest floor and make use of another gift given them by Kehtean.

When the next morning comes, they gather quahog clams from the bottom of the bay and sickissuog clams from the shore when the tide is low. Then, from the shallow water, they gather great loads of a seaweed called rockweed. The

rockweed is covered with chambers filled with gas, and the body of the plant contains a great deal of salt water. When the fire for the clambake has burned down to ashes and the Rock People are glowing with heat, that rockweed is piled on top of the stones. Steam begins to rise as the salt water in the plants boils, and the clams, along with lobsters and corn, are piled onto the rockweed and then covered with more armfuls of seaweed. The *Appanaug* is part of the great Medicine Circle of life, one of the gifts of the Great Spirit. So, as the food cooks, the people say prayers of thanksgiving to remember all the gifts they have been given. It is the way it was done long ago and it is still done that way today.

Note: A wonderful book about the Wampanoag tradition of the clambake has been written by Russell Peters, a Wampanoag elder whose Indian name is Fast Turtle. A former president of the Mashpee Wampanoag Tribal Council, Fast Turtle tells the story of how he and his grandson, along with other tribal members, prepare one such great feast in his book *Clambake, A Wampanoag Tradition* (Minneapolis, Minn.: Lerner, 1992). A videotape that follows every step of the clambake has also been made. It is called *Appanaug.* It was Fast Turtle who first told us the tale of Maushop and his Wampanoag friends.

Steam begins to rise as the salt water in the plants boils.

Fallen Star's Ears

Long ago, a woman married a star. She lived in Sky Land for a while, but grew homesick for her people. She made a rope and tried to lower herself and her little baby down to the ground, but her rope was not long enough and she was not strong enough to climb back up. She held on for a time and then fell. It was a long fall and the young woman was killed, but her baby survived.

The birds and animals cared for the boy, and when he was grown, he went to look for his people. Because he came from Sky Land, he became known as Fallen Star, and many things happened to him as he traveled along.

One day, Fallen Star was traveling along in the wintertime. Near dusk, as he was passing through a stand of alders, he saw smoke rising and climbed a hill. From that hilltop he could see a village. Below him, looking down into that camp, stood a very big man. Around that man's neck was a necklace made of human ears.

"I have heard of that man," Fallen Star said. "That is Double Face."

"Creep inside,"
Fallen Star said.
"All is ready."

Fallen Star went back down the hill until he came to the stand of trees. He picked the bracket fungus from those trees and shaped them with his knife so that they looked just like ears. Then he strung them about his neck and walked back over the hill to the place where Double Face still stood.

As soon as Double Face saw the necklace worn by Fallen Star, he greeted him. "Friend," Double Face said, "you are welcome. Have you come to help me kill those people in that village below?"

"It will be easy to kill them and take their ears," Fallen Star said. "Do those people know how to kill men like us?"

Double Face laughed. "No," he said. "None of them know that all they have to do to kill me is to trap me so that I cannot run away. Then, if they throw buffalo grease in the fire and shake a buffalo horn rattle I will die."

"Those people are foolish," Fallen Star said, "but I will help you kill them. I will go down and see if they are asleep. If they are asleep, I will make a call like an owl. Then you can creep into that big lodge and take their ears."

"That is a good plan," said Double Face. "I will wait for you to call me."

While Double Face waited, Fallen Star went down into the village. He went into all the lodges and warned the people.

"The one who kills the people and takes their ears is here," Fallen Star whispered. "Make a fire and be ready with buffalo grease and a buffalo horn rattle."

Then Fallen Star made the sound of an owl. Double Face came creeping down into the village and found Fallen Star waiting in front of the big lodge.

"Creep inside," Fallen Star said. "All is ready."

As soon as Double Face was inside the lodge, Fallen Star closed the door flap and laced it tight. Double Face tried to get out, but Fallen Star held the door shut.

"Throw the grease into the fire! Shake the medicine rattle!" Fallen Star shouted.

The people did as he said. As soon as the grease struck the fire it flared up high. Inside the big lodge, Double Face screamed. Then they shook the medicine rattle made of buffalo horn and Double Face's screams stopped. The one who killed the people and took their ears was dead. Then, because he had other places to go and more things to do, Fallen Star left that village. But ever since then, the fungus which grows on the trees has looked just like human ears.

Fallen Star held the door shut.

Koluskap and Malsom

L ong ago, before there were human beings, Koluskap and his brother Malsom lived together on the island of Oktomkuk. They were giants and both of them had great power. Because of his nature, Koluskap always tried to do things which would make life better for others. And because of his nature, Malsom always did things which made life difficult for everyone.

When Koluskap made the rivers, he made them so that one bank flowed downstream and the other flowed up-stream. That way, the people yet to come would find it easy to travel. But Malsom threw stones into the rivers, twisted their courses and made them all flow downstream.

Next Koluskap made all kinds of flowering and fruiting plants. He made beds of moss which would be soft places for people to sleep. But Malsom followed behind him and made plants which had thorns and plants which were poi-sonous, and he made the moss so moist that the people would grow cold if they tried to use it as a bed.

Then Koluskap began to make the fish. He took great care with them and the last one he made he tried to make the

There stood an
animal unlike
any of
the others.

best of all. But Malsom came along, stepped on that last fish and flattened it out so that it was no longer so beautiful. Today that fish is the flounder.

One day, as Koluskap was walking around, he decided to make animals. He picked up some earth and shaped it in his hands and spoke the names of the animals as he shaped each one.

"Moose," Koluskap said, and the first moose stood there.

"Mooin," he said, and Mooin, the bear, was made.

So he continued, shaping the deer, the squirrel, the rabbit and many others. But as he did this, hidden among the tall ferns, Malsom watched him. Malsom did not have the power to shape things, but he did have the power to twist Koluskap's creation.

As Koluskap began to shape the last handful of earth, Malsom whispered a word from his hiding place before Koluskap could speak.

"Lahks," Malsom whispered. And as he whispered that word, the earth in Koluskap's hand twisted and fell to the ground. There stood an animal unlike any of the others. It was smaller than Mooin, yet it was fiercer than the bear and had great strength. It was shaped a bit like the beaver, but its teeth were pointed and sharp and its eyes gleamed in a way unlike any other animal. It was Lahks, the wolverine.

As soon as he had been made, Lahks began to try to make things difficult. He went to Moose and spoke to him. "If you meet a human being," he said, "you must pick him up with your sharp horns and throw him high in the air."

Moose listened and went along his way until he came to Koluskap. "Koluskap," said Moose, "I know what I must do. If I meet a human being, I must pick him up with my long, sharp horns and throw him up into the air."

Koluskap shook his head. "Nda," Koluskap said, "you must not do that. If you meet a human being, you must run away."

Then Koluskap reached out his hands and made Moose smaller and then flattened its horns so they would no longer be so sharp and dangerous.

One after another, Lahks went to the animals, telling them what they should do. In those days, Squirrel was as large as the bear is today.

"You must grab the human beings and tear them apart," Lahks said to Squirrel.

But Koluskap was following behind Wolverine. When Koluskap came to Squirrel, he picked Squirrel up and stroked him until Squirrel became as small as all squirrels are to this day.

Next Lahks went to Bear, who was twice as large as bears are today. "When you see a human being, you must swallow him," Lahks said.

Lahks began to try to make things difficult.

But Koluskap followed behind the wolverine. He made the bear smaller and closed his throat tighter so that Mooin's food would be small things and not human beings.

Malsom watched all this from his hiding place among the ferns, and he was not pleased. So he went to Koluskap.

"Older Brother," Malsom said, "I know that you have great power. But is there not something which can kill you?"

"Younger Brother, it seems that I might be killed by an owl feather," Koluskap said.

That night, while Koluskap slept, Malsom crept off and found an owl feather. He came back and struck Koluskap on the head with it. But all that it did was to wake Koluskap.

"Younger Brother," Koluskap said, "why are you tickling me?"

"Older Brother," Malsom said, "you were having a bad dream and so I decided to wake you."

The next day, Malsom asked Koluskap again. "Older Brother," he said, "is there nothing that can kill you?"

"Younger Brother," Koluskap answered, "it seems that I might be killed by a cattail."

That night, as Koluskap slept, Malsom crept up to him with a large cattail in his hand. He struck Koluskap on the head with it and the fluff of the cattail scattered as he struck.

"Ah-ha!" Malsom said, "I have broken his head."

But then Koluskap sat up. "Younger Brother," he said, "what is wrong?"

"Older Brother," Malsom said, "you cried out in your sleep and so I decided to wake you."

So it went on, with Malsom trying to find the way to destroy his brother and Koluskap never telling him how to do it. One day, however, as Koluskap sat by the river which ran through the hills, he thought he was alone.

"My brother does not know," Koluskap said, speaking to the sky, "that I can be killed only by a blow from a flowering rush."

But Koluskap was not alone. Lahks, the wolverine, was hiding in the tall ferns, and he crept to the place on the other side of the hills where Malsom sat.

Malsom, too, thought he was alone. "Ah," Malsom said, speaking to the sky, "I have tried and tried to find what will destroy my brother. But he does not know that the only thing which can destroy me is a blow from the root of a fern."

Then Lahks came out of his hiding place. "Malsom," he said, "will you give me whatever I ask for if I tell you the one thing which can defeat your brother?"

Then Lahks came out of his hiding place.

"I will give you whatever you ask," Malsom said, leaping to his feet. "Now tell me quickly."

"Koluskap can be destroyed by striking him with a flowering rush," Lahks said. "And now you must give me what I want. I want to have wings so that I can fly like the hawk."

But Malsom laughed at Lahks. "What need do you have for wings?" he said. Then he went off to find a flowering rush.

Lahks was angry. He went as quickly as he could to Koluskap. "I have told your brother what can defeat you. He is looking now for a flowering rush," the wolverine said. "But the one thing which can destroy him is the root of a fern like those all around us!"

Then Koluskap reached down and pulled out a fern root. As he did so, Malsom came running down the hill with a flowering rush in his hand, ready to strike his brother and destroy him. But Koluskap struck first with the fern root. As soon as it struck Malsom, he was defeated. Malsom fell and was changed into a long mountain range.

So it happened long ago. And though Malsom has gone from the world, Wolverine still goes about making things difficult for everyone. And those mountains, which are called the Long Range, are still there in northwestern Newfoundland.

The panther
and the owl
had not slept.

Why Some Trees Are Always Green

When the plants and animals were first made, they were told to watch and stay awake for seven nights. All of the animals and plants wished to do this. They knew if they did not sleep, they would be given some special sort of power.

The first night passed and all of the animals and plants stayed awake. It did not seem hard to them and some of the animals and plants even began to boast about how easy it was.

When the second night came, it no longer seemed so easy for all of them and some found it very hard not to fall asleep. When the next night came, some of them could stay awake no longer, and by the fourth night, nearly all of them slept.

When the seventh night ended, only a few had stayed awake. Among the animals, only the panther and the owl had not slept. So they were given the power to see in the dark. From then on, the panther and the owl would be able to prey on those animals which had failed to remain awake and watchful and now must sleep each night.

Among the plants, only the pine, the spruce, the hemlock, the cedar, the laurel and the holly had remained awake and watchful. Because they were faithful, they were given the power to remain green all year around, and their leaves would hold great medicine. But all of the other plants would have to lose their leaves each winter because they did not endure the test. Not only that, but they would also have to fall asleep until the warmth of spring came again.

So it is that to this day when young men go out to fast on a hill and pray for their medicine, they remind themselves they must stay awake like the cedar and the spruce and the pine. They must look into the dark with the vigilant eyes of the panther and the owl. For great medicine never comes to those who are not watchful.

When the seventh night ended, only a few had stayed awake.

The Bitterroot

It was the time just after winter in the valley in the mountains. There was no food and the people were starving. The fish had not yet returned to the streams and the game animals had moved far away into the mountains. The men had gone out to seek game and they had been gone a long time. It was not yet time for berries to ripen, and the women had gathered what plants they could find that could be eaten, but the ones that were left from the winter were tough and stringy.

In one of the lodges, an old woman was grieving because there was no food for her grandchildren. She could no longer bear to look at their thin, sad faces, and she went out before sunrise to sing her death song beside the little stream which ran through the valley.

"I am old," she sang, "but my grandchildren are young. It is a hard time that has come, when children must die with their grandmothers."

As she knelt by the stream, singing and weeping, the Sun came over the mountains. It heard her death song and it spoke to that old woman's spirit helper.

The old woman looked and it was as the bird said.

"My daughter is crying for her children who are starving," Sun said. "Go now and help her and her people. Give them food."

Then the spirit helper took the form of a redbird and flew down into the valley. It perched on a limb above the old woman's head and began to sing. When she lifted her eyes to look at it, the bird spoke to her.

"My friend," the redbird said, "your tears have gone into Earth. They have formed a new plant there, one which will help you and your people to live. See it come now from Earth, its leaves close to the ground. When its blossoms form, they will have the red color of my wings and the white of your hair."

The old woman looked and it was as the bird said. All around her, in the moist soil, the leaves of a new plant had lifted from Earth. As the sun touched it, a red blossom began to open.

"How can we use this plant?" said the old woman.

"You will dig this plant up by the roots with a digging stick," the redbird said. "Its taste will be bitter, like your tears, but it will be a food to help the people live. Each year it will always come at this time when no other food can be found."

And so it has been to this day. That stream where the old woman wept is called Little Bitterroot and the valley is

also named Bitterroot after that plant, which still comes each year after the snows have left the land. Its flowers, which come only when touched by the sun, are as red as the wings of a red spirit bird and as silver as the hair of an old woman. And its taste is still as bitter as the tears of that old woman whose death song turned into a song of survival.

It will be a food to help the people live.

Indian Summer

Here lives my story. It happened long ago that there was a man named Zimo who was a good planter. He cared well for his crops and he gave thanks to Ketci Niweskwe. But when the time came for him to do his planting, he became sick. The other people of his village planted their crops and harvested them and dried them for the winter, but Zimo remained sick all through that time. The other people of the village and their families had plenty of vegetables, but Zimo had none. The first cold winds of late autumn were blowing and he knew it would be hard to survive the winter without the food he always got from his fields.

So Zimo went to Gluskabe.

"Master," Zimo said, "I have been sick. The time came to plant and then the time to harvest and now I have no food for the winter. I have always been thankful, and I have worked hard in the past. Help me."

"Go back to your field," Gluskabe said. "Plant your seeds."

"Master,"
Zimo said,
"I have
been sick."

Zimo did as Gluskabe said. The people of Zimo's village thought he was crazy as he began to plant his corn and squash and beans. But as soon as he put the seeds in the earth, the weather changed and it became as warm as summer. The seeds sprouted and grew tall overnight. By the time seven days had passed, Zimo had gathered a whole season's crop. Then winter came.

Since then, though the seeds no longer grow as quickly as Zimo's seeds did with the help of Gluskabe, there is always a time of warm weather just before the snows. That is the time the Penobscot people call "A Person's Summer." It is known to most as "Indian Summer," even though few seem to remember that it is a time given as a reminder to us all to be thankful for the gifts from Earth and the Creator.

*The basket
came with her,
carrying
her load.*

The First Basket

In the old days, it was hard work for the women when they went to gather food on the prairie. Not only did they have to walk far from their villages to dig for roots, but they also found it hard to carry the food they found back to their earth-lodges. One day, long ago, a woman sat down to rest under a cedar tree. She leaned back against its trunk, and the sound of the wind in its branches was so peaceful that she fell asleep. And as she slept, the cedar tree spoke to her.

"Sister," the cedar tree said, "I see that you are tired and I want to help you. Do as I say and good will come to you and to all the women of your people. Dig down into the earth beneath you. Take my slender roots and weave them together. They will help you carry your load."

When the woman woke, she did as the tree had told her. She uncovered the long, thin roots with her digging stick and cut them free with her flint knife. Then, remembering that she should show her own thanks because she had been given a gift, she placed some tobacco and then filled the hole back in with dirt. Then she took the roots and wove them

together as she had been shown in her dream. When she was finished, she had the first cedar basket, and she saw that it would be good to carry things. It was light and strong.

The woman had been digging tipsin roots before she rested and now she went back out onto the prairie and loaded all of the tipsin into her cedar basket. But when she tried to lift the basket, she began to weep.

"This basket is so heavy," she said, "and I am so tired now."

Then the cedar basket spoke to her.

"Sister," said the basket, "do you not remember the words my mother spoke to you? Did she not say that good would come to you? Did she not say that I would help you? If you will sing as you walk back to your lodge, then I will carry this load."

The woman stood and began to sing as she walked back to her lodge. The basket came with her, carrying her load.

When the women of the village heard that song coming from the prairie, they came out of the village to see why someone was so happy after a day of hard work. When they saw the woman's basket carrying her load, it filled them with wonder.

"Where did you get this basket?" they asked her.

"It is your job to carry my load," the woman said.

"The cedar tree showed me how to make it," the woman answered.

Then all the women begged her to show them how to do the same. Soon, every woman in the village had her own basket made of cedar roots, and at the end of each day the voices of singing women could be heard as they returned from the prairie with their baskets beside them, carrying the loads.

One day, though, a woman took her basket out on the prairie, and as she dug, she found there a granary of the Mouse People. The Mouse People gather the beans and seeds of the prairie plants and store them underground for their winter food. It was the practice of the Mandan people, when they found one of these granaries, to always leave some behind so that the Mouse People would not starve. This woman was greedy, however, and filled her cedar basket to the top, taking all of the beans and seeds which the Mouse People had worked so hard to gather. In the tall grass, the Mouse People were crying, but this woman paid no attention.

However, when she stood up from filling her basket, this greedy woman found that she could not remember the song to sing to make the basket carry her load. She ordered the basket to carry her load, but the basket did not move. Even when she struck it, the basket remained on the ground.

"It is your job to carry my load," the woman said.

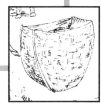

But the basket did not answer her. That woman, in her greed and anger, had forgotten that what the cedar baskets did for the people was done out of kindness. Because of the way she acted, the basket became resentful. It refused to carry her load. Because the load was too heavy for her to carry, she had to pour out most of the beans and seeds she had taken from the Mouse People. After that woman had gone, the Mouse People took those beans and seeds to a new and better hiding place.

And from that time on, no basket ever again carried a load on its own for the people.

But the basket did not answer her.

Blue Dawn

I n a house, they say, lived Black Cane Old Man; Old Corn Woman, his wife; their daughter, Yellow Corn Girl; and their small son, Blue Dawn. Black Cane Old Man was the one in the pueblo whose work it was to bring the rain.

Each day, although Old Corn Woman was blind, she would work at her loom. While her mother worked, Yellow Corn Girl ground corn and her little brother, Blue Dawn, played *huib*, a game where you run and kick a stick ahead of you as you go. Blue Dawn's uncle, Nachuruchu, was a great *huib* player and Blue Dawn wanted to be as good as his uncle at running. Each day, as Blue Dawn played his game, an eagle watched him and wanted the boy for her own.

To make sure she knew where her small son was, Old Corn Woman always kept him tied to the end of the long belt she was weaving. One day, though, she no longer heard the sound of his running. She pulled the belt back in and Blue Dawn was gone. The eagle had come and stolen her child.

Blue Dawn became human from the top of his head to his neck.

"Come here," she called to Yellow Corn Girl. "Hurry! I don't know where my little child is."

Yellow Corn Girl came out and searched for her brother but she could not find him. She asked all the people of the pueblo, but no one had seen him. The village crier went about telling all the people to look for Blue Dawn. But the little boy was nowhere to be found.

All the people were sorry. Black Cane Old Man no longer was able to work to bring the rain. Now the rain did not come. Now the corn all got dry. Now all the people knew they would be hungry, for without the rain they would have no crops.

One day, Nachuruchu, the uncle of Blue Dawn, rose at dawn and began to play *huib*. He kicked the stick ahead of him as he ran. He ran far from the pueblo. He ran up high into the mesas. Then, sometime in the middle day, as he ran he heard a song being sung by a child. It came from high on the top of a cliff which no one could climb.

> Che-e mah-weh, mah-weh
> Che-e mah-weh, mah-weh
> I am the little son of Black Cane
> I am the little son of Black Cane

When Nachuruchu heard this he stopped to listen.

"That is no other but my little nephew," he said.

Back to the pueblo Nachuruchu ran.

"My nephew was carried away by the eagle. I heard him singing from the top of the high place where no one can reach. That is why we have not been able to see him."

"Go back again at dawn," Nachuruchu was told by the old men, the fathers of wisdom. "See if you hear the same song again."

Nachuruchu did as the people said. He went again to that mesa at dawn, and again he heard the voice of his nephew singing.

Now the people knew where Blue Dawn had gone. The young men were sent out. They tried to climb that cliff to reach him, but the cliff was too steep.

As they tried, the Stone-Layers, the swallows who make their nests out of clay, were flying around them.

"Bird-Masons," the young people called to the swallows, "what payment do you want to help us bring our small child down from the cliffs up there?"

But the swallows were flying and calling out, "Chee-Chee," and did not hear the people. Up and down the swallows went, calling out, "Chee-Chee! Chee-Chee!"

The people kept calling to them and at last one swallow heard the people. "Listen," he said. "Someone is talking."

But the little boy was nowhere to be found.

Then the swallows listened and heard the people asking them what payment they would ask to bring the human child down from the cliffs.

"We will take pine nuts," the swallows said. "You can give us pine nuts to bring down your child."

All the swallows flew up and tried to lift Blue Dawn down from the eagle's nest. But the boy was too heavy.

"We are sorry," they said, flying back to the people. "We tried but we could not lift your child."

But because the swallows had tried their best, the young men still gave pine nuts to the swallows.

Then the birds spoke among themselves. "Let us go to Grandmother Spider," they said.

When they came to her house, Grandmother Spider was waiting. She said to them, "What is it that you want?"

The swallow told her about Blue Dawn. Grandmother Spider listened closely.

"So it is?" she said. "My poor grandson is crying? Grandsons, let us eat first and then we will see what I can do."

With that, Grandmother Spider served up atole and acorn mush for the swallows in dishes made of acorn shells.

Together, Grandmother Spider and the swallows ate. Then, when they had thanked her for the food, Grandmother Spider took one of her baskets.

"Now," she said, "I will go to see what I can do."

Soon they came to the mesa where the young men were waiting at the bottom of the cliff. As soon as they saw Grandmother Spider, they called to her.

"Our Grandmother, will you help us? Will you bring our child down from way up there?"

"Yes," Grandmother Spider said. "I will do this. But take care not to look up."

Then Grandmother Spider went up the cliff with her basket. She found Blue Dawn and put him into her basket.

"Here he is!" she called and began to lower him.

But, as soon as she said that, the young men looked up. When they looked up, a wind began to blow and it lifted the basket back up into the air.

"Do not do that!" Grandmother Spider called down.

"Grandmother," the young men called back, "we will not look up again."

Then Grand-mother Spider went up the cliff with her basket.

Now Grandmother Spider hung the basket down. She lowered the basket down to the young men. But when the young men looked into the basket, they did not see a little boy. Instead, they saw only a young eagle.

The young men carried the eagle child back to the pueblo. The fathers of wisdom came and looked at the eagle child.

"This is Blue Dawn," they said. "We must make him a human being again."

For four days the fathers of wisdom went without food. Then they began to work wisdom. They set the eagle child down. They sang. As they sang the first words, they rolled the Ma-koor hoop. As they did so, Blue Dawn became human from the top of his head to his neck. They sang a second time and rolled the Ma-koor hoop. Now Blue Dawn became human down to his waist. They sang a third time and rolled the Ma-koor hoop. Now Blue Dawn was human down to his knees. A fourth time they sang and rolled the Ma-koor hoop and Blue Dawn was human down to his ankles. A fifth time they sang and rolled the Ma-koor hoop and it was done. It was finished.

They warmed water then and made Blue Dawn drink. After drinking the water he began to cough. Each time he coughed, the food he had eaten as an eagle child came from his mouth. He coughed and lizards came out, snakes came out, rabbits came out, mice came out. All that the eagles had fed him came from his mouth as he coughed. When this was done, the fathers of wisdom gave Blue Dawn back to his parents.

Black Cane Old Man came and picked up his son and embraced him. Old Corn Woman and Yellow Corn Girl embraced Blue Dawn. They carried him back to their home. Now Black Cane Old Man could work again to bring the rain. Rain began to fall. In the fields, the corn came up. The corn blossomed and it ripened.

Now the *Cacique*, the chosen leader of the people, told them it was time to pick the corn. The village crier proclaimed that it was time to pick the corn. The people went out into the fields and picked. They brought the corn into the house of the Cacique. The house was filled and there was still more corn left over.

"Go to the east," the Cacique said. "Go to the north. Take the corn through the streets. From northwest to west, from west to south, from south to east, take this corn through the streets and give it to all the people."

So it was that the people of Isleta were glad and lived well. *Ta-kee-whee kay-ee*.

They carried him back to their home.

Survival

He saw that
her feet sank
into the earth
with each step.

The Woman Who Lives in the Earth

The animals, the birds, the lakes and trees, even the grass—all these have something alive which dwells within them. The Chugach people call this the *shua*. And Earth itself, on which life depends, also contains a *shua*. The Chugach call this being *Nunam-shua*, the One Who Lives Within the Earth, and she is seen as a woman.

This woman who lives within the Earth also has her home in the stones and the plants. Sometimes she is known as The One Who Dwells in the Alder Trees, but she also can walk the land in the shape of a woman. A bright light shines all around her when she walks. She wears boots made of the fur of all the animals of the land. She wears a long coat, which hangs down to her knees, hangs as lichen hangs on the stones. On her coat are many tiny animals: the caribou, the arctic fox, the musk ox, the wolf, the bear, the lemming and the hare. These are the souls of the animals which she protects, all of the animals of the land. Those animals all came originally from Earth.

The people, too, came from Earth. The first children, the Inuit say, were formed out of Earth in the places where the small willow trees grow. They were covered by the willow

leaves and the soil gave them food. So the human beings must always be careful what they do on Earth. They must remember Nunam-shua.

One day, during the time when the caribou migrate, a hunter went out to seek game. As he walked, he was careful where he stepped so that he did not scrape the lichen off the stones. When he moved through a thicket of small alder trees, he bent the branches gently so that they did not break. Soon he came upon the caribou herd and he stalked closer. He was careful in his movement and so was able to come very close to the caribou without frightening them. He watched them for a long time, picking out the ones which were cows with calves and the ones which were leading the herd. Those were the animals which he knew should not be killed. He chose the animal he wished to take and then spoke to its spirit as he pulled back the arrow in his bow. His shot was a good one and the animal fell dead. He could have shot more animals, but he did not need them. So he put down his weapon, took his pouch from his side and went to the fallen caribou. Before he began to cut it up, he thanked the animal's spirit for giving itself to him. Then he placed something in its mouth to show his gratitude. As he skinned and butchered the animal, he wiped his hands on his own clothing and not on the grass, remembering that the grass is sacred at the time when the caribou migrate.

This hunter did not know it, but everything he did had been watched by Nunam-shua. He became aware of a light and turned to see a woman walking toward him. The air shone all around her and as she walked he saw that her feet

He bent the branches gently so that they did not break.

sank into the earth with each step. He was afraid, because he knew who this was. He knew the power of The Woman Who Dwells in the Earth. Not long ago, a man had been cutting a live alder tree and had fallen dead. The people knew that he had died because Nunam-shua lived within the alders and the man had shown no respect for the tree while cutting it.

Nunam-shua came close to the man and stopped. She looked straight into the hunter's face and he looked down at Earth to show respect.

"You have done well, child," she said to him. "You hunt the animals with care. You do not show contempt for the grass and the trees and Earth. So I give you these."

Then Nunam-shua reached up and took from her coat tiny animals in the shape of the caribou, the musk ox and the hare. The man held out his hands to take those tiny animals. As soon as he touched them, they melted like snow into his hands. When he looked up, Nunam-shua was gone. But because she had given him the gift of those animal spirits, a gift which had entered into him like rain into the soil, from that time on he was always successful whenever he hunted the animals of the land.

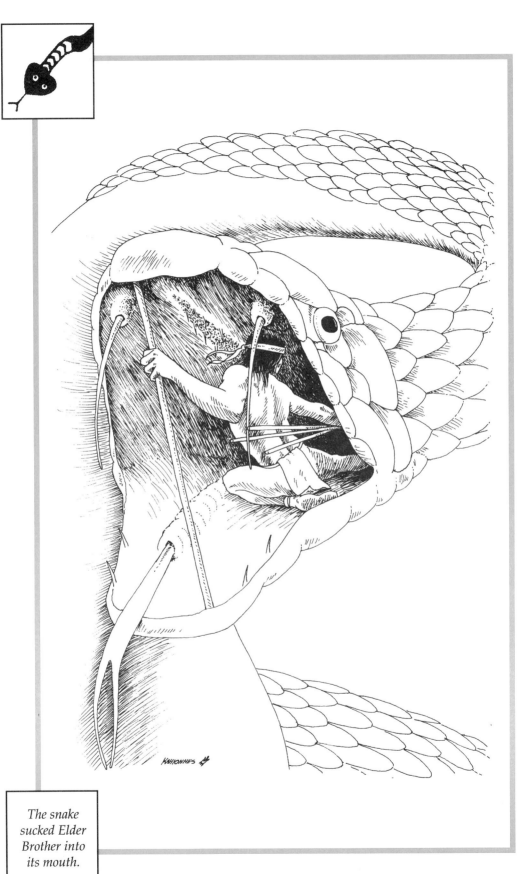

The snake
sucked Elder
Brother into
its mouth.

Waw Giwulk: The Center of the Basket

S h hab wa chu'i na'ana. They say it happened long ago. All was well with the O'odham, the People. All was in harmony. But then a great snake came from out of Earth. It came to the place where the people lived and began to devour them. It sucked the people into its mouth. Those people who escaped the great snake called to Itoi, Elder Brother.

"Help us!" they called.

Itoi came then from his home on Waw Giwulk. He came from his house in the center of the world.

"Give me an obsidian knife and four greasewood sticks," Elder Brother said.

Then Itoi took the knife and sticks and went to meet the great snake.

The snake sucked Elder Brother into its mouth, but he stuck the first greasewood stick into the snake's mouth and wedged it open. It sucked him down into its throat, but he

stuck the second greasewood stick in the great snake's throat and wedged it open. It sucked him down into its esophagus, but he stuck the third greasewood stick in and held its esophagus open. It sucked him down into its belly, but he wedged in the fourth greasewood stick and held its belly open.

In the great snake's belly, Itoi listened. He listened for the sound of its heart. With his obsidian knife he slashed the heart and then ran out of the great snake, pulling free each greasewood stick as he ran. So Itoi killed the great snake.

Elder Brother went back to the O'odham and told them the danger was over. Then he went back to his home on Waw Giwulk. *Am o wa'i at hoabdag.* That is at the center of the basket.

So Itoi killed the great snake.

How Fox Brought the Forests From the Sky

In the old days, pine and fir and spruce and cedar trees could not be found on Earth. They were all kept in Sky Land by Moon. Moon was the chief of Sky Land.

One day, Moon decided that he would like to have some way to get down to Earth below. So Moon spoke to Spider.

"Make me a rope that will reach down to the top of those mountains."

Then Spider wove a rope which stretched from the clouds down to the mountains below. Then Moon closed the clouds at the top so that no one else could use that rope to get up into Sky Land.

But Blue Jay had sharp eyes. Blue Jay saw that rope leading down from the sky and told Fox. Blue Jay and Fox waited until it was a night when there was no moon, and then they went up that rope till they came to the bottom of the sky. Then, with his strong beak, Blue Jay pecked a hole in the clouds and the two entered the land in the sky.

*They went up
that rope till
they came to
the bottom
of the sky.*

While Blue Jay waited in a tree, Fox decided to look around. Before long, Fox found a lake and saw that someone had placed a trap in it to catch beavers.

"This is Moon's trap," Fox said. Then he made himself into a beaver and climbed into the trap.

When Moon came to check his trap the next morning, Moon was pleased.

"I have caught a fine beaver," Moon said. Then he carried the beaver back to his smokehouse, skinned it and threw the carcass into the corner. As soon as night came and Moon went to sleep, Fox came back to life. He pulled his skin from the wall, put it back on, went outside and looked around. There were trees everywhere: pine trees, fir trees, spruce trees, cedar trees. There were no trees like those in the world below. Fox used his spirit power. He pulled up many trees and made them so small he could carry them under his arm. Then he went back to the place where Blue Jay still waited in a tree near the hole in the sky.

"Quick," Blue Jay said, "Moon is waking up."

But Fox was still in the shape of a beaver, and he used his sharp teeth to weaken the rope which reached down to the mountains below. Then, he and Blue Jay climbed down the rope and reached Earth below. When they were far enough away, they watched to see whether Moon would follow them.

Moon was not far behind. When he woke he saw that the beaver skin was gone, and he found footprints leading away from his smokehouse.

"One of the Below People has tricked me," Moon said. He followed the footprints and came to the hole which led to the mountains below. Moon began to climb down the rope, but before he had gone far, his great weight was too much for the weakened rope to hold. The rope broke, and Moon fell down to Earth below. As soon as he struck the ground he was changed into a mountain. That mountain is Mount Si and you can still see the face of Moon on its side.

Fox and Blue Jay then went to work. They planted the trees all over the mountains. That is why, to this day, there are forests of spruce trees and fir trees and pines and cedars all over the Cascade Mountains.

Moon fell down to Earth below.

The People of Maize

(Adapted from the Popul Vuh *and Lacandon Maya traditions.)*

The Creator and the Maker, Tepeu and Gucumatz, made people first out of earth. Out of mud they made the flesh of human beings. But it was not good. The mud was soft and it melted away. The people made of mud had no strength and they fell down. Their sight was blurred, and they could not move their heads to turn them or to look behind. These people of mud spoke, but they had no minds. The water soaked them and they could not stand.

Tepeu and Gucumatz said, "Our creatures will not be able to walk. They will not be able to multiply. Let us try again."

Then they broke up the people made of mud and returned them to Earth, to the living Earth.

Then they did a divination to see how they should make the people. And the divination said that it would be well to carve people out of wood.

So the Creator and the Maker carved people out of wood. They took the wood from the rainforest and they said,

These new people were made out of maize.

"These figures of wood will speak, they will walk about Earth."

And the people made of wood stood up and walked about. They looked like people and they spoke like people. They increased in number and spread about the land. They hunted the animals and they worked the earth. They made clearings in the rainforest to plant their milpas where their food plants could grow. But these people of wood did not have souls. They did not have minds. They had no blood and their cheeks were dry. Their feet and hands were dry. Their knees would not bend and they made no offerings. They did not offer incense to the gods. They continually hunted the animals without mercy. They continually cut the trees of the rainforest without showing thanks. They had no thought for the Creator and the Maker, for those who had created and cared for them. They did not speak with the Creator and the Maker.

So a great flood was sent down by the Heart of Heaven on the heads of the people made of wood. The face of Earth became dark. Black rain fell by day and by night. Then Xecotcovach, the great eagle, flew down to strike at the eyes of the people of wood. Camalotz, the great bat, flew down to strike at their heads. Cotzbalam, the jaguar who waits, came roaring to eat them. Tucumbalam, the tapir, came running to trample them.

Next the small animals and the large animals came to attack those people made of wood. The sticks and stones flew up to strike the people made of wood. Everything

began to speak, even the water jugs and the clay plates and the grinding stones.

"You hurt us and you did not thank us," the dogs and turkeys and hens said. "You beat us and ate us, and now we will kill you."

"You tormented us every day," the grinding stones said. "You scraped our faces: *holi, holi, haqui, haqui*. Now that you are no longer human beings we will grind you up."

Some of the people made of wood tried to run away. They climbed to the top of their houses, but their houses fell down. They ran into the rainforests and climbed into the trees, but the trees threw them down. They tried to go into the caves, but the caves cast them out. At last, almost all of those people made of wood were destroyed and their villages were no more. Again the rainforest grew where their milpas had been. Only a few of those original people survived, and they became the howler monkeys who live in the rainforest.

Finally, the Creator and the Maker, Tepeu and Gucumatz, decided to try once again to make human beings. They held council to decide what would be used to make the flesh of the people. They did a divination and were told to ask help of four animals. Those four animals, the parrot, the jaguar, the coyote and the crow, told them of the yellow ears of corn and the white ears of corn. They showed the Creator and the Maker the road to Paxil. They brought the Creator and the Maker to Paxil where the corn grew.

Now they would not forget to take care of the rainforest.

The Creator and the Maker ground that corn and made it into dough. From that cornmeal dough they fashioned the flesh, the arms and legs and the bodies of the people. It was the blood of these new people. These new people were made out of maize.

The people made of maize were intelligent and far-seeing. They were thankful. They sang and praised the Creator and the Maker. They sang and praised the forest and the animals. But the people made of maize could see too far. They could see all of Earth and all of heaven. They saw so far that the Creator and the Maker became worried that these new people would become arrogant. So they darkened the eyes of the new people. Now the new people could no longer see into the farthest heavens. Now their sight was limited to the closest parts of Earth and Sky. Now they would not become arrogant and forget to be thankful. Now they would not forget to take care of the rainforest. The people made of maize would only remember how far they had once seen when they offered incense in the ceremonies and when they gave thanks to those who made them. As long as they remembered to give thanks and to take care of the forest, all would be well for them. So it remains to this day.

There were
many seeds
on that
tall grass.

Waynabozho and
the Wild Rice

One day, when Waynabozho was out walking around, his grandmother called him to her lodge.

"Grandson," Nokomis said, "it is time for you to go to some distant place in the forest and fast. Then a dream may come to you to help the people yet to come."

But Waynabozho did not like the idea of walking so far.

"I will go in my canoe," he said. Then he began paddling along from lake to lake.

Waynabozho had not gone far when he saw tall grasses growing from the shallow waters at the edge of the fourth lake he entered. He liked the way that tall grass looked. There were many seeds on that tall grass, and he took a big piece of birch bark and made it into a basket. Then he used a stick to knock off many of those seeds into his bark container. When he was done, he took the seeds back to his grandmother.

"Look what I have found," he said. "The tall grass that held these seeds is very fine to look at. Let us plant these

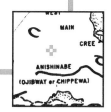

seeds along the shores of our own lake so we will have those grasses to look at from our lodge."

Nokomis did as Waynabozho asked. She helped him scatter the seeds along the edge of the lake.

"Now Grandson," she said, "you must continue on your way. You must go out and fast and hope that something good will be given to you."

So Waynabozho set out again in his canoe. He went from lake to lake and then he just leaned back in his canoe and let the boat drift. "I can wait here for a dream," he said. "Why should I trouble myself to walk?" He went without food all the rest of that day.

"This fasting is easy," Waynabozho said. "I will surely have a strong dream come to me soon." But no dream came and he fell asleep as he drifted along in his canoe.

The next day came and when Waynabozho woke up he was unable to think of anything but food. He felt hungrier than he had ever felt before. As the canoe drifted along he saw some plants growing along the shore.

"Boozhoo, Waynabozho," the plants said. "Helloo! Are you hungry? You can dig one of us up and eat the root. Then you will no longer be hungry at all."

"Ah," Waynabozho said, paddling his canoe quickly to the shore. "This must be the vision I was waiting for. I have

She helped him scatter the seeds along the edge of the lake.

fasted a very long time. I must do as these plants tell me to do." Then he began to dig up the plants. He did not just dig up one, he dug them all and ate their roots.

But when Waynabozho was finished eating, he began to feel very sick. Just as the plants had said, he was no longer hungry at all. He became so sick that he could not move. He lay there for three days and three nights. Finally, on the fourth day, he found enough strength to drag himself back into his canoe and paddle weakly toward home.

But when he was within sight of their lodge, he saw new plants growing from the shallow water of the lake.

"Waynabozho," these new plants said, "sometimes we can be eaten."

Carefully, Waynabozho picked some of the seedheads of those plants. He sprinkled some of the seeds back into the water before he ate. Those plants tasted good and he no longer felt weak and sick after eating them.

"What are you called?" he said.

"We are manomin," said the wild rice plants. "You are the one who planted us here. Do you not remember?"

Then Waynabozho collected many of the seedheads of the wild rice, leaning the plants over and scraping them gently with a stick as he had done before. He made sure to let some of the seeds go into the water as he did this. That is

how wild rice is gathered to this day by the Anishinabe. And as Waynabozho paddled home he knew that he would have much to tell his grandmother. He had succeeded in his quest. He had found something good for the people yet to come.

He had
succeeded
in his quest.

Healing Our Relations

"I will be
a great symbol
for you, Little
Ones," the Bull
Buffalo said.

The Buffalo Bull and the Cedar Tree

When the Osage people came down from the sky, they wandered the world seeking guidance and help. They wanted to learn the right ways to live and they trusted the beings they met to guide them.

The first being they met was the great Bull Buffalo. It lowered its head and bellowed with anger. It pawed the earth, throwing up red dust. Then a man of the Peace Clan fired an arrow. That arrow was fletched with Eagle's down feathers, feathers stained red with pokeberry juice to make them a symbol of peace and the dawn. The arrow entered the open mouth of the Buffalo Bull and that great one grew quiet from the magic of peace.

"I will be a great symbol for you, Little Ones," the Bull Buffalo said. Then it rolled on the ground four times. Each time it rolled, thunder rolled overhead. Then, where it had rolled, healing plants grew. The green gourd and the yellow striped gourd, the poppy mallow and the blazing star grew up from the earth where the buffalo rolled.

"I give these plants for you to use," the Buffalo Bull said to the people. "Use them and you will see old age as you travel the path of life."

"Of what will our children make their bodies?" the people asked.

Then the Buffalo Bull made the red corn grow. Then the Buffalo Bull made the red squash grow. The Buffalo Bull made blue corn and black squash. The Buffalo Bull made speckled corn and speckled squash. The Buffalo Bull made yellow corn and yellow squash.

"When your children use these plants as food, they will see old age. They will reach the days when life is filled with calm and peace."

So the Buffalo Bull said to the people. Then he told the Osage, "You may have my body. You may use it for food, shelter, clothing and tools."

As the people continued to travel on, they saw the leaves falling from the trees. They had come to the earth in the time of autumn. They continued to travel and the days grew colder and now all of the trees were bare of leaves. But then they came to the edge of a cliff and there before them they saw a tree whose boughs were still green. Its scent was fragrant. It was Cedar. They looked at that tree and, as she stood in the midst of the four winds, sending forth her fragrance whichever way the wind blew, she spoke to them.

They saw a tree whose boughs were still green.

"I stand here on this cliff," Cedar said, "so that the Little Ones may make of me their medicine. Look at my roots, a sign of my old age. When the Little Ones make me their symbol they, too, will live to see their toes gnarled with age. Look at my branches, how they bend. With these as symbols, the People will live to see their own shoulders bent with age. Look at the feathery tips of my branches. When the Little Ones make these their symbols, they will live to see their own hair white with age as they travel the Path of Life."

So it was that the Osage people accepted the cedar tree as their symbol of the Tree of Life.

Glossary and Pronunciation Key

The following rules are used for the phonetic description of how each word is pronounced:

1. A line appears over long vowels. Short vowels are unmarked. For instance, "date" would appear as dāt, while "bat" would appear as bat.
2. An accent mark (´) shows which syllable in each word or name is the one emphasized.
3. Syllables are broken with a hyphen (-).
4. Syllables are spelled out as they are pronounced. For instance, "Cherokee" appears as chair-oh-key.

Where appropriate, the culture from which each word or name comes is given in brackets [ ], followed by the meaning of that word or name or an explanation of its significance as it appears in the text.

Aataentsic (Ah´-tah-en-sik) [Huron]. "Ancient Woman."

Abenaki (Ab´-er-na-kee or Ab´-eh-na-kēē). People living at the sunrise, "People of the Dawn." A northeastern Algonquian group.

Algonquian (Al-gon´-kee-en). Large, diverse grouping of Indian peoples related by a common linguistic root. Algonquian Indians live in the Atlantic coastal regions from what we now call the Maritime Provinces to the southeastern United States, west to the Prairie Provinces and down through the central states into Wyoming and Montana.

Am o wa'i at hoabdag (Am oh wah´ee at ho-ahb-dahg) [O'odham]. "That is at the center of the basket."

Anishinabe (Ah-nish-ih-nah´-bey) or Anishinabeg. The Native people found in the central and northern Great Lakes areas of North America. They are the same people known as the Ojibwa and the Chippewa, names applied to them in the past few centuries and used widely today by Anishinabe people themselves. *Ojibwa* (O-jib´-i-wah) was a name given them by their neighbors and probably means "Those Who Make Pictographs." *Anishinabe* means "First Men" or "Original Men." *Chippewa* is a variant of Ojibwa. (Ojibwa is also translated as "puckered up," referring to their moccasin style, which is puckered in front.) Currently the Anishinabe are one of the largest Native groups, with a U.S. and Canadian population of more than 160,000.

Aniyunwiya (Ah-nee-yoon-wi´-yah). The Cherokee people, whose original homelands included the areas now known as Tennessee, Kentucky and North Carolina. *Aniyunwiya* means "Real People." *See* Cherokee.

Appanaug (Ahp´-puh-nawg) [Wampanoag]. "Clambake" or "seafood cooking."

Cacique (kah´-seēk). Spanish word used to refer to Native chiefs in areas now or formerly dominated by the Spanish, as among the Pueblos of the American Southwest. Origin is Native West Indian, from the Arawak word *kassequa*.

Camalotz (Kahm-ah´-lots) [Maya]. "Great Bat."

Cherokee (Chair-oh-kēy´). Corruption of a Lenni Lenape [Delaware] Indian name (*Talligewi* or *Tsa la gí*) for this very large southeastern tribe who called themselves *Aniyunwiya* (Ah-nee-yoon-wi´-yah)—"Real People." One of the so-called (by whites) Five Civilized Tribes. *See* Aniyunwiya.

Cheyenne (Shy-ann´). Name commonly used for the northern plains Native people who call themselves *tsitsitsas*, "The Striped Arrow People." From the Dakota word *shalyena*, meaning "Those Who Speak Strangely."

chief. This is one of the most widely used and misunderstood words applied to Native people today. All too often, every Indian man is called "Chief " by non-Indians. In some cases, this can be seen as an insult, especially if that man is *not* a chief. Other Native men, who, indeed, are "chiefs," do not mind having that word applied to them. Early Europeans thought a "chief " among the Native peoples of the Americas was like a king, and they even called many traditional leaders "king" (e.g., King Philip, who was known as Metacomet by his own *Wampanoag* [Wom-pah-nō´-ag] people). In general, a chief was a person chosen by his people to lead them. He was not all-powerful and the roles of such chiefs varied widely from one part of North America to another. In many tribal nations, if a chief did not behave properly, he was taken out of office by the people. Sitting Bull once explained that a chief, by definition, has to be a poor man because he must share everything he has. "Chief," therefore, is not a term to be used lightly.

Chippewa (Chip´-ah-wah). *See* Anishinabe.

Chugach Inuit (Chew´-gatch). Inuit people in the area of Alaska near present-day Anchorage.

circle. The circle is seen as a special symbol for many Native people. It is continuous and all-embracing. When people gather and form a circle, the circle can always be made larger to include more. Those who sit in the circle are all at the same height, and all are the same distance from the center—thus it promotes and stands for equality. The "Sacred Hoop" referred to by many of the Native people of the plains is another vision of the circle and stands for life itself, continuing, never-ending, as well as standing for "the nation."

clan. Among most Native peoples the concept of "clan" exists. A term also applied to Scots and other European peoples, *clan* refers to groups of people within a nation who are "born into" a particular group, though they are not necessarily related by blood. Among the Mohawk there are three clans—

Turtle, Wolf and Bear. A person *always* belongs to the clan of his or her mother. If a person from another nation (including a white person) entered a tribal nation, that person had to be adopted by a clan mother and was then of her clan. Among many Native nations, people were not supposed to marry someone of their own clan. Further, if a member of the Bear Clan among the Mohawk, for example, met a person of the Bear Clan from another Native nation, she or he might regard that person as a sister or a brother. Clans, therefore, created links among people and nations, as well as a sense of belonging to a special group.

clan mother. Elder woman regarded as the head of a particular clan. Among matrilineal people such as the Haudenosaunee (Iroquois), a clan mother has great power and is a major political force. Among the Haudenosaunee, the women have a strong, central role. Each clan is headed by an elder woman, a clan mother, chosen by the others of her clan to lead. The clan mothers and the other women of the clan have many duties— such as choosing the men who will be "chiefs" among the Haudenosaunee. If a Haudenosaunee chief does not do his job well, the clan mother warns him three times and then, if he still fails to behave appropriately, she takes away his chieftaincy. The roles of clan mothers varied, and in some Native nations of North America there were no clan mothers per se.

Cotzbalam (Kohts´-bah-lam) [Maya]. Jaguar Chief.

da neho (dah ney-hō´) [Seneca]. Literally, "It is finished." A conventional way to end a story among the Iroquois.

Delaware. *See* Lenni Lenape.

Eskimo (Es´-kih-mō). Cree word meaning "Fish Eaters," applied to the people who call themselves *Inuit*—"The People." *See* Inuit.

Fast Turtle. Wampanoag name for Russell Peters, a contemporary Wampanoag elder.

Gitchee Manitou (Gih-chēē´ Man´-ē-too) [Anishinabe]. The Great Spirit.

Gluskabe (Gloos-kah´-bey) [Abenaki]. "Storyteller," the trickster and changer hero who lived on Earth before the human beings.

Grandmother. The term *grandmother* is used among many Native people to refer in a respectful way to a female elder, whether human or animal.

Grandmother Spider. Grandmother Spider is a central character in many stories of the U.S. Southwest. She is seen in some stories as the Creator of many things. She introduced weaving to the people, and the rays of the sun are sometimes seen as part of her great web. She is a benevolent force in the Native world of such people as the Diné (Navajo) and Pueblo nations.

Great League [Iroquois]. The alliance of peace forged among the formerly warring five nations of the Iroquois about 500 years or more ago by The Peacemaker and Hiawatha; also known as the League of Peace. The Great League is still active among Iroquois peoples.

Great Mystery or Great Spirit. A translation of various Native names for the Creator, such as the Anishinabe term *Gitchee Manitou* or the Abenaki term *Ktsi Nwaskw* (T-see´ Nah-wahsk´).

Gucumatz (Goo´-koo-matz) [Maya]. The Maker.

hageota (hah-gey-ōh´-tah). Iroquois word for a person, usually a man in middle age, who travels from lodge to lodge telling stories and being rewarded for his efforts by being given small gifts, food and a place to stay.

Haudenosaunee (Ho-dē-nō-shōw´-nē) [Iroquois]. Iroquois name for themselves, which means "People of the Longhouse."

Hiawatha (Hi-ah-wah´-tha) [Mohawk]. One of the historical founders of the League of the Haudenosaunee.

holi, holi, haqui, haqui (ho-lee´ ho-lee´ hah-key´ hah-key´) [Maya]. Words imitating the sound of a grinding stone.

huib (weeb) [Isleta Pueblo]. Game played by running and kicking a stick.

Huron (Hyu´-ron). A Native people of the St. Lawrence Valley and Ontario region of present-day Canada. Name drawn from the French *hure*, "disheveled head of hair."

Itoi (Ē´-ē-tōy) [O'odham]. Elder Brother, Our Creator.

Inuit (In´-you-it) [Eskimo]. "The People," name used for themselves by the Native peoples of the farthest Arctic regions, Iceland and Arctic Asia. Not regarded by themselves or Indians as North American Indian.

Iroquois (Ear´-oh-kwah). Corruption of an Algonquian word *ireohkwa*, meaning "real snakes." Applied commonly to the Six Nations, the "Haudenosaunee." *See* Haudenosaunee.

Isleta Pueblo (Is-leht´-ah Pweb-lo). One of the oldest of the Pueblo communities, located just south of present-day Albuquerque, New Mexico.

Kahionhes (Gah-hē-yōn´-heys) [Mohawk (Iroquois)]. Name meaning "Long River."

Kanietakeron (Gah-nee-dah-gay´-loo). This traditional name for David Kanietakeron Fadden, who was born in the month of March, means "Patches of Snow." A member of the Wolf Clan from the Mohawk community of Akwesasne, he is a museum educator at the Iroquois Indian Museum in Howes Cave, New York. In addition to stories illustrated for *Keepers of Life* and *Native Plant Stories*, his work has appeared in *Keepers of the Night*, *Keepers of the Animals* and various Native publications including *Akwesasne Notes*, *Indian Time* and materials for the Six Nations Indian Museum, where he works to preserve Haudenosaunee traditions.

Kehtean (Kay´-tyahn) [Wampanoag]. "Great Spirit."

Ketci Niweskwe (kuh-tsee´nah-wah´-skwah) [Micmac]. "Great Mystery."

Kishelemukong (Kish-luh´-moo-kong) [Lenni Lenape]. "Great Spirit."

Koluskap (Kōh-loos´-kahp) [Micmac]. *See* Gluskabe.

Lacandon Maya. Native people of the highland jungles of Chiapas province in Mexico.

Lahks (lahx) [Passamaquoddy]. "Wolverine," who is a dangerous trickster figure.

Lenni Lenape (leh-nee´ lay-nah´-pee). "We, the people," the name that the people sometimes called Delaware, whose traditional lands include present-day New Jersey and Pennsylvania, call themselves. Many Lenape now live in Oklahoma, having been forcibly resettled there almost two centuries ago.

longhouse. Large traditional dwelling of Iroquois people. Framework of saplings covered with elm bark with central fires and, to each side, compartments for families.

Malsom (mahl´-sum) [Micmac]. "Wolf."

Manabozho (Man-ah-bō´-zo). Algonquian trickster hero, "Old Man."

Mandan (Man´-dan). An agricultural people of the Great Plains whose traditional homelands are in North Dakota.

manomin (mah-no´-min) [Anishinabe]. Wild rice.

Maushop (Maw´-shop). Culture hero of the Wampanoag people.

Maya (My-uh). A Native people of Mexico and Central America.

medicine. As this word is used in contemporary Native cultures it refers both to medicinal preparations used for curing illnesses and to things that may bring good fortune or a certain kind of power.

milpa (mihl-pah) [Mayan]. A cultivated field in the rainforest.

Miwok (Mee´-wohk). Native people of the part of California surrounding the San Francisco Bay area and east of the bay.

Mohawk (Mo´-hawk). From an Abenaki word indicating "enemies." The Mohawk are the easternmost of the Six Nations of the Iroquois, the "Keepers of the Eastern Door." Their name for themselves is "People of the Land of the Flint."

Mooin (moo´-in) [Micmac]. Bear.

nda (un-dah´) [Abenaki]. No.

Nokomis (Nok-kōh´-miss). Anishinabe term for grandmother; grandmother of Manabozho in stories.

Nunam-shua [Chugach Inuit]. "The Dweller in Earth."

Oglala Lakota (Ō-glo´-lah Lah-ko´-tah). One of the branches of the western Lakota (Sioux) people.

Ojibwa (Ōh-jib´-wah). *See* Anishinabe.

Oktehrakenrahkowa (Ohk-dey-lah-gen-lah-gō´-wah) [Mohawk]. "Great White Root," one of the four roots which must be followed to bring people together in harmony under the Great Tree of Peace.

Oktomkuk (ohk-tahm´-kook) [Passamaquoddy]. Island off the coast of Maine.

Onondaga (On-un-dah´-gah) [Iroquois]. The centralmost of the six nations, the "Fire-keepers." Name for themselves is *Onun-dagaono*, "People on the Hills."

O'odham (Ōh-ōh´-dum). Southwest Indian group of southern Arizona. Nomadic horticulturalists and prolific basket weavers. Two-thirds of the roughly 13,500 Papagos today live on reservations located mostly in Pima County, Arizona, with some living in Sonora state, Mexico. Sometimes referred to as *Tohono O'odham*, "People of the Desert." *See also* Pima.

Osage (Ō´-sāj). The people who call themselves *Ni-U-kon´-Skah*, "The People of the Middle Waters." Their lands formerly included the area where Missouri, Kansas, Arkansas and

Oklahoma meet, but today their communities are mostly in Osage County, Oklahoma.

Palenque (pah-len´-kay). Ancient Mayan city famous for its pyramids, in the current state of Chiapas in Mexico.

Papago (Pah´-pah-gō). *See* O'odham.

Passamaquoddy (Pass-uh-mah-kwah´-dee). Wabanaki nation of the eastern coast of Maine. Their name comes from *Peske-demakddi,* "plenty of pollock."

Penobscot (Pen-ahb´-skaht). Wabanaki nation of southern Maine. Their name comes from *Penaubsket,* meaning "it flows on rocks."

Peters, Russell (Fast Turtle). [Wampanoag]. Author and former president of the Wampanoag Indian Tribal Council.

Pima (Pee´-mah). Native people of the Sonoran Desert region of present-day Arizona and Mexico who call themselves *Akimel O'odham,* "River People." The name "Pima" appears to originate from a phrase the O'odham used to answer the many questions asked them by the Spanish, *"Pi nyi maach,"* which means "I don't know." *See also* O'odham.

Popponesset (Pah-po-nah´-sit). A bay off the coast of Martha's Vineyard in Massachussetts.

Pueblo (Pweb´-lō). Spanish for "town," refers to a number of "town-dwelling" Native peoples along the Rio Grande in New Mexico who live in large adobe buildings like apartment complexes.

Salish (say´-lish) [Okanagan]. Sometimes called "Flatheads," the Salish are one of the divisions of the Okanagan peoples of the Pacific Northwest. Okanagan (oh-kah-nah´-gun) is usually translated as "People Who See to the Top."

Seneca (Sen´-eh-ka). Corruption of Algonquian word *O-sin-in-ka*, meaning "People of the Stone." Refers to the westernmost of the Six Nations, "Keepers of the Western Door of the Longhouse." The Iroquois who called themselves *Nundawaono*, "People of the Great Hill."

Sh hab wa chu'i na'ana (shuh-hab wah chu´ēē nah´-ahnah). This means, "They say it happened long ago" in O'odham.

shua (shoo´-ah) [Inuit]. The living spirit that dwells within all life.

sickissuog (sik´-ih-soo-ahg) [Wampanoag]. "Clams that spit."

Sioux (Su). *See* Dakota. Corruption of an Anishinabe word meaning "Snakes," which refers to those who call themselves *Dakota* or *Lakota* or *Nakota* or *Ocheti Shakowin* (Oh-che-ti Shah-ko-win), "The Seven Council Fires."

Snoqualmie (Snōw-kwal´-mē). One of the Native peoples of present-day Washington.

Sonkwaiatison (Son-kway-ah-dee´-sō) [Seneca]. The Holder-Up of the Heavens, the Creator.

Ta-kee-whee kay-ee (tah-key´-whee kay´-ee). Formulaic way of ending an Isleta Pueblo story, roughly meaning "that is all."

Tepeu (Tey´-pyu) [Mayan]. "The Creator."

tipsin root. A member of the pea family with a large root the size of a hen's egg used widely as a food by the Native peoples of the Great Plains.

tribe. From Latin *tribus*. A term used by both Indians and non-Indians to refer to groups of Native North Americans sharing a common linguistic and cultural heritage. Some Native North American people prefer to speak not of "tribe" but of *nation*.

Tsalagi. *See* Cherokee.

Tucumbalam (Too-coom-bah-lahm´) [Mayan]. "Tapir."

Tuscarora (Tus-ka-rō´-rah). The Sixth Nation of the Iroquois. The name means "Shirt-wearers." Driven by the Europeans from lands in North Carolina in the early eighteenth century, they resettled in western New York State.

Wabanaki Confederacy (Wa´-bah-na-kēē). A loose union of a number of Abenaki nations circa 1750–1850, possibly echoing an earlier confederacy and influenced by the Iroquois League. Allied Micmac, Maliseet, Passamaquoddy, Penobscot and

Abenaki nations. Wampum belts were introduced and triannual meetings held at Caughnawaga, Quebec.

Wampanoag (Wom-pah-nō´-ag). Means "Dawn People"; sometimes called *Pokanoket*. Algonquian linguistic group of eastern woodlands who once occupied what are now Bristol County, Rhode Island, and Bristol County, Massachusetts. Many were killed, along with the Narragansetts, by the colonists in King Philip's War in 1675 (King Philip was the colonists' name for Chief Metacomet, son of Massasoit). At least 500 Wampanoag live today on Martha's Vineyard, Nantucket and other places in the region.

Waw Giwulk (waw gee´-woolk) [O'odham]. "The center of the basket."

Waynabozho (Way-nah-bō´-zo). *See* Manabozho.

Xecotcovach (Hey-kot-kō-vatch) [Mayan]. "Great Eagle."

Zimo (zee´-moh) [Abenaki]. "The Planter."

Tribal Nation Descriptions

Anishinabe (Ah-nish-ih-nah'-bey)

The Anishinabe, or "The People," are also known as the Chippewa (in the United States) or the Ojibwa (in Canada), names which may refer to the puckered style of moccasins they wear. They are a people of the Great Lakes Region in the center of the continent and they speak an Algonquian language. Their houses were called wigwams. Most wigwams were single family dwellings, dome-shaped structures of bent and tied poles with bark covering. Very large lodges, shaped something like an Iroquois longhouse were also used for special ceremonial purposes, such as the meetings of the members of the Midewiwin, a medicine society whose members had to devote their lives to serving the good of their people. (*Mite wiwin* means "medicine dance.") Elaborate pictographs drawn on birch bark were used by members of the Mide Society to remember songs and other texts.

Every Anishinabe person also belonged to a clan or "totem." Among many tribal nations, a person always belongs to the clan of his or her own mother. However, among the Anishinabe, clan was inherited from the father's side and, like the Iroquois, these clans were usually named after animals or birds and you were never supposed to marry someone from your own clan.

Anishinabe material culture was based on the forest. Wood was used to make bows and arrows, bowls, snowshoes, flutes, drums, lacrosse sticks and many other things. Their baskets, the covering of their homes and the skins of their canoes were of birch bark and much of their food was gathered from the forest, requiring them to live a seminomadic life. In the early spring, around March, they would set up camp near the groves of maple trees to tap them for sugar , boiling the sap down in big wooden troughs. In the summer they would live in small villages where they did some gardening, gathered wild food and fished, ranging over an area with a radius of forty miles or more. In the fall, they moved to the rivers and lakes where the wild rice was now ripe and spent several weeks harvesting it. To this day, Anishinabe people harvest the wild rice. In the winter, they moved to their hunting grounds, where the animal they most relied upon for food and for their clothing was the deer.

Their central culture hero is called Manabozho and there are hundreds of stories about him. In some stories he is heroic and in others he acts foolishly—teaching proper behavior by showing what happens when you do the wrong thing. Manabozho is the actual hero of Longfellow's epic poem *Hiawatha*. Unfortunately, Longfellow mistakenly used the name of the Onondaga man who helped the Peacemaker found the League of the Iroquois. Making a historical Iroquois figure into a mythic Anishinabe hero is like telling the story of the Norse God Thor and calling him Charlemagne! (Sadly, mistakes such as Longfellow's can be found in many books about Native people.) Today, the Anishinabe are among the most numerous of the Native people of North America, with about 160,000 living in communities in Michigan, Wisconsin, Minnesota, North Dakota and Southern Ontario. Some live on reservations, such as Turtle Mountain, White Earth and Leech Lake, but large communities of Anishinabe also exist in such cities as Minneapolis and St. Paul.

Cherokee (Chair-oh-kēy′)

The name the Cherokee use for themselves is *Aniyunwiya*, which means "the principal people." They also call themselves Tsa-la-gí (which became "Cherokee"), derived from the Choctaw chiluk-ki, which means "Cave dwellers." The Cherokee, along with the Choctaw, the Chickasaw, the Creek, and the Seminole (who were, themselves, a branch of the lower Creek Nation), were called the "Five Civilized Tribes" because they sucessfully adopted white ways. The fact that they were only called "civilized" because they had taken on certain culture traits from the European-based immigrants is an expression of the ethnocentric attitudes toward Native people held by the white culture.

Their homeland was the central Appalachian mountains. They lived in large villages along the banks of the rivers. Each village had a large council house and a central plaza for political meetings and ceremonies. Their individual homes and the council house were usually made of wattle, woven saplings covered with mud. The conical Cherokee house was called the *asi*. In the summer, the Cherokee people would move out of their wattle houses to live in open-sided shelters. The typical head-covering for a Cherokee man was not a feathered cap, but a wrapped turban, sometimes decorated with one or more tall feathers.

Like their northern cousins, the Iroquois, the Cherokee people were matrilineal and matrilocal. They also relied upon the deer and corn as their main sources of food. They closely observed the animals of the forest, and in many of their stories, like the tale of the Possum, those animals gather together in council just as the Cherokee do.

Of the southern Native nations, the Cherokee was the largest. In the 1700s, their lands covered 70 million acres across what is now Tennessee, Georgia, Alabama and North Carolina. By the late 1700s, they had given up their old style of house and adapted to white ways. A man named Sequoia codified the Cherokee language (using, some say, a script in use since pre-Columbian times by Cherokee medicine people) and by 1820, more than half of the 17,000 Cherokee could read and write their own language. Aside from using their own language and keeping certain of their customs, the Cherokee were hard to distinguish from their white neighbors. They had newspapers, banks, schools, farms, wore white clothing and got along well with most of their non-Indian neighbors.

What happened next is one of the saddest stories in American history and a shameful one. Gold was discovered on Cherokee land in 1827. The state of Georgia then claimed the Indian lands as part of its state wealth. The Cherokees were ordered to leave and the other states of the south did the same to the other four Civilized Tribes. Led by Chief John Ross, the Cherokee fought the case in the courts. In the end, the U.S. Supreme Court decided that removal of the Cherokee was not legal. They had a right to remain on their own land. Shamefully, President Andrew Jackson supported the Indian Removal Act of 1830. "The Supreme Court has made their decision," President Jackson said, "now let them enforce it."

Some Cherokee went voluntarily to the land designated as Indian Territory (the current state of Oklahoma). More than 15,000 refused to leave. Finally, in 1838, soldiers were sent to forcibly remove the Cherokee from their homes, their farms and their lands. More than 4,000 Cherokee died along the way to Oklahoma on what came to be called The Trail of Tears. Among those who died was Quatie Ross, the wife of the principal Cherokee Chief, who gave her blanket to a freezing child.

A number of Cherokee people escaped into the hills of North Carolina. As a result, the Cherokee nation of today is divided between the Cherokee of Oklahoma and the smaller Eastern Band of Cherokee in North Carolina, which numbers about 6,000. Other Cherokee people and their descendents are scattered all over the face of the continent. The majority of Cherokee, more than 50,000 by the last census, live in Oklahoma, which became the United States dumping ground for many other dispossessed tribal nations throughout the 1800s. (In the last act of betrayal, even "Indian Territory" was taken from the Indians in the early 1900s and made into the state of Oklahoma.) The Cherokee Nation of Oklahoma has its capital in Tahlequah. The tribal offices there provide information to visitors about their heritage center and festivals open to the public. The Eastern Cherokee offer much to visitors who come to Cherokee, North Carolina, including a museum, a reconstructed village, craftspeople demonstrating and selling their traditional works and an annual pageant offered all summer called "Unto These Hills," portraying the history of the Cherokee.

Cheyenne (Shy-ann')

The Cheyenne people, who are an Algonquian people, call themselves *Dzi tsi stas*, which means "people alike." The name Cheyenne comes from a Lakota word *Sha-Hi-yena*, which means "our allies." The Cheyenne have also been known as the "Striped Arrow

People," due to their preference for turkey feathers to fletch their arrows. Prior to 1700, the Cheyenne lived in Minnesota, where they were primarily agriculturalists. Their neighbors to the east were the Sioux and when the Sioux were pushed west when their eastern neighbors the Anishinabe obtained guns from European traders, the Cheyenne were forced farther west, onto the northern plains. There, with the introduction of the horse, they created an entirely new culture, based not on farming, but on following the great buffalo herds as hunters. They also became friends with another tribal nation, the Sutaio, who brought with them the ceremony of the Sun Dance. At some point, within the last 200 years, the Sutaio were incorporated into the Cheyenne tribe.

Around 1851, the Cheyenne nation was divided into two parts—the Northern Cheyenne and the Southern Cheyenne. Both communities exist to this day, with the Northern Cheyenne based in Montana and the Southern Cheyenne in Oklahoma. Frequent allies of the Lakota, the Cheyenne were known to be brave fighters in defense of their people and their land and it is estimated that, in proportion to their population, they suffered more casualties than any of the other plains nations. The Southern Cheyenne were driven from Colorado after the notorious massacre of a peaceful village of Cheyenne and Arapaho people at Sand Creek in 1864. Ironically, the same village of Cheyenne people suffered another massacre at the Washita River in Oklahoma at the hands of Custer in 1868.

The Northern Cheyenne Council, in Lame Deer, Montana, holds an annual pow-wow each July and runs a tribal museum which presents their history and culture. The Cheyenne-Arapaho Business Committee, located in Concho, Oklahoma, has an annual pow-wow over Labor Day.

Haudenosaunee (Hō-dē-nō-shōw'-nē)

The Haudenosaunee or Iroquois. An early confederation of five Native Nations, the Iroquois had highly developed diplomacy and what might be called an "international culture." Iroquois traditions speak of migration from the west to their present homes in the areas now known as New York State, and the Canadian provinces of Ontario and Quebec.

The five original nations were the Mohawk, the Oneida, the Onondaga, the Cayuga and the Seneca. When their lands were taken from them by white settlers, the Tuscarora people migrated north from North Carolina and were allowed to join the Iroquois League as the Sixth Nation. Their confederacy was known as the Great League and it was symbolized by a giant white pine tree, the Tree of Peace. On the top of the tree, an eagle perched watching for any threat to the peace, holding five bundled arrows—a symbol of strength in unity—in its claws. (That same symbol of the eagle and the bundled arrows is found on the U.S. quarter—borrowed from the Iroquois, whose league is now credited by many historians as having a direct influence on the formation of American democracy and the Constitution.)

The Iroquois relied on both agriculture and hunting to feed their people. Their stories and ceremonies of Thanksgiving (instead of one Thanksgiving, the Iroquois have Thanksgiving several times throughout the year, each ceremony at a time when some event in the natural world—such as the ripening of the corn or the gathering of maple syrup—deserves thanks) honor both the animals and the plants.

The dwellings of the Iroquois people were called Longhouses. (Haudenosaunee means "People of the Longhouse.") The longhouses were often huge in size, their roofs taller than two men, buildings big enough to hold as many as twenty or more families in apartments on either side of the central fires. Long inner walls running north to south created a corridor in the middle. The arched roof was vented with smokeholes for the central fires, which provided heat in the cold seasons and were used by everyone for cooking. Typically, a longhouse was inhabited by the people of a single clan and headed by an elder Clan Mother. There were many clans among the Iroquois, named after the birds and animals who were regarded as friends and relations of the people. The three clans found among all of the five Iroquois Nations were Turtle, Bear and Wolf.

Among the Iroquois—and most other Native nations in North America—women were very powerful and equal to the men in terms of influence and respect. Iroquois women were responsible for agriculture and were the owners of the longhouses. Clan was inherited from the mother's side (making them matrilineal), and when a man married he went to live with his wife's clan. (This made them a matrilocal people—residency controlled and decided by the mother's side.) The women also decided which of the men of their clan would represent them as Faithkeepers (the equivalent, one might say, of senators or representatives) at the meetings of the Great League. If a man did not behave properly when he was a representative, the women of his clan would warn him three times. After the third warning, the woman would symbolically "remove his horns," taking him from office. Because the Great League was a League of Peace, formed long ago by a man known as The Peacemaker at a time when the Iroquois nations were fighting each other, no representative to the League was allowed to fight in war and anyone who had been a warrior could never be a Faithkeeper.

Huron (Hyu'-ron)

The Huron people, close relative of the Iroquois, are a confederacy of four tribes whose traditional homeland is present-day southern Ontario in Canada. Their name for themselves is Wendat, which means "People Living on the Island." The name Huron was given them by the French and is derived from the word "hure," which refers to their traditional way of wearing their hair in a stiff ridge on top of the head. As with their Iroquois neighbors, most of their food came from farming, with corn as the main crop. It is estimated that they numbered about 20,000 in the early 1700s, living in large villages with 1,000 or more people in each. Since their homeland is estimated to have been only about 700 square miles, they were clearly very successful farmers.

Allies of the French, the Huron and Iroquois alike became dependent on European trade goods. Wars over the control of trade resulted in the complete defeat of the Huron at the hands of the Iroquois in 1649, at which point the Huron abandoned their homeland and were dispersed. Some settled among the Iroquois and others went northeast to seek sanctuary with the French, where one branch of the Huron found a permanent home near the Jesuit mission of Lorette, eight miles north of Quebec. That reserve, which became known as Wendake, was reduced over the years to its present size of about 150 acres. The Huron who went west became known as the Wyandot. Their travels over the next two centuries took them from Wisconsin, Michigan and Ohio through Kansas to their present-day home in Oklahoma in the late 1800s. The Wyandot Tribe of Oklahoma is based in Wyandotte, Oklahoma, in the northeastern part of the state

Inuit (In'-you-it)

Inuit (who call themselves Inupiaq or Inupiat in Alaska) live in the far north. Many families have relatives on both the Asian and the North American sides of the Siberian land bridge that used to span the strait between the two continents. The Inuit people are found widely across the far north, including Siberia, Alaska, Canada and Greenland.

Although the Arctic climate is harsh—a land of no trees and, where there is earth, the ever-present permafrost is only a few inches below the surface even at the height of summer—the Inuit live full lives in balance with their environment. These Native people of the far north distinguish themselves from the "American Indian," regarding themselves as being of another race. Inuit or Inupiaq is a word meaning "real people." They have also been popularly called "Eskimo," a name first applied to the eastern Canadian Inuit by the French in 1584 and spelled "Esqui-maux." Eskimo is a word which apparently comes from an eastern Algonquian language, and the exact meaning of it is not clear, though it may refer to the making of snowshoes. The word does not mean "raw meat eaters," though the *Oxford English Dictionary* tells us this.

The Inuit people are found in a band of habitation which stretches across northern Asia and Northern America, including Greenland, where they were called not Eskimos but "Greenlanders" for many centuries before Columbus came to America. There are many different Inuit groups around the Arctic, with differences in the dialects they speak. However, they recognize their kinship and in 1977 at the Inuit Circumpolar Conference in Alaska adopted the name "Inuit" to apply to all peoples once called "Eskimo."

A knowledge of the animals of ocean and land is vital for survival in the far north, as is an attitude of respect and gratitude. When an Inuit hunter spears a seal, he will fill his mouth with fresh water and then give that water to the dead animal, in the belief that it has allowed itself to be killed in exchange for that drink.

The efficient clothing of the Inuit, their methods for hunting caribou, seal, walrus and whale; their shelters built of driftwood, whalebones, snow and ice; their dog sleds; even a type of "sunglasses" worn to screen their eyes from the glare of the ice and avoid snowblindness—have all been developed over thousands of years as a result of surviving by living close to nature. Though there are cultural differences over the broad expanse of their region, which spans the vast northern edges of two continents and one great island—America, Asia and Greenland—there are many distinctively Inuit practices. These include methods of winter travel over tundra and sea ice, hunting and fishing techniques for capturing marine and land animals, specialized tool designs, unique social customs and strong oral traditions. They are well known for their use of skin boats, harpoons, oil lamps and spear throwers. Their beautiful carvings of stone and walrus ivory and bone are now seen in galleries all over the world, and it has been widely acknowledged that their shamans show a deep knowledge of the human psychology and of effective medical practice.

The major comings of European culture to the Inuit probably began with a colony founded by the Norse in Greenland in the year 982. Subsequent changes, especially in the twentieth century, have brought certain conveniences to the Inuit peoples such as outboard motors, rifles, snowmobiles and radios, but have also brought social and economic influences which have disrupted the pattern of their cultures. The development of oil resources in

Alaska has also brought many formerly isolated communities into regular contact with western civilization. However, the contemporary Inuit people are attempting to survive by combining the new with the old and by making their reliance upon nature and their respect for it a central part of their new way of life. Inuit groups from all over the Arctic meet regularly at Inuit Circumpolar Conferences, which are held in different locations each year. These meetings consider such things as the continuance of the Inuit way of life and the threats to the fragile environment of the far North being posed by western development and pollution.

Iroquois (Ear'-oh-kwah)

See *Haudenosaunee*.

Isleta Pueblo (Is-leht'-ah Pweb-lo)

Isleta, with more than 3,000 people, is the largest of the Tiwa-speaking Pueblo communities in present-day New Mexico. The various comunities of peoples, who live in compact villages made up of multilevel "apartment" buildings made of wood, stone and adobe bricks, were first called "Pueblos" by the Spanish in the sixteenth century. Most of the Pueblos are along the Rio Grande, as is Isleta itself, which is made up of several settlements near the river. Three different language groups are found among the Pueblos: Keresan, Tanoan and Zuni. Tanoan itself is broken down into three dialects: Tiwa, Tewa and Towa.

The nineteen villages of the Pueblo peoples are one of the oldest civilizations in North America. Many of their settlements have been occupied continuously for hundreds of years, and the agricultural methods they have developed to grow corn in dry soil are extremely sophisticated. Historically peaceful, the Pueblo people were brutally colonized by the Spanish. Although the Pueblo settlements staged a successful rebellion against the Spanish in 1680 under the leadership of a San Juan Pueblo man known as Popé, the Spanish managed to regain control again by 1696. From that point on, however, the Spanish changed their tactics, abolishing many of the harsh practices which led to the revolt.

Despite centuries of foreign domination, the Pueblos have maintained their languages and their ceremonies, many of which are still forbidden to outsiders. By carefully choosing which new things to adopt, the Pueblos have managed to adapt to cultural change. The result is, as Alfonso Ortiz, the San Juan Pueblo historian puts it, "that modern Pueblos retain traditional values and close communities."

Isleta is the farthest south of the Pueblos along the Rio Grande, thirteen miles below Albuquerque. Vistors are welcome and can purchase permits for camping and fishing at Isleta Lakes, owned by the Pueblo.

Lenape (Lay-nah'-pee)

Sometimes known as the Lenni Lenape, which translates as "We, the People." The traditional homeland of the Lenape people is along the East Coast, between the river valleys of the Hudson and Delaware rivers, including the area now known as New York City. The two major divisions of the Lenape were those who lived to the north and spoke the Munsee dialect and those who lived to the south and spoke Unami. First known by the Europeans as "River Indians," they were given the name "Delaware" in the 1600s after the English named one of those rivers the Delaware after Thomas West, the Baron de la Warr.

As was true with their nearby Algonquian relatives (and frequent allies) the Mahicans and their neighbors, the Haudenosaunee, the Lenape were excellent farmers raising corn, beans, squash and other plants. Like many of the other Native nations of the East Coast, the Lenape were displaced by the Europeans and were forced to migrate many times. They are, perhaps, the most dispersed of all the surviving Native nations. Despite this, the Lenape have always shown the ability to adapt and survive. When, for example, their reservation in Kansas was sold in 1866, 1,000 "Delawares" resettled among the Cherokee in Oklahoma. Although listed as a part of the Cherokee Nation, the Oklahoma Lenape strongly maintain their own identity and have a tribal office in Anadarko, Oklahoma. Some Lenapes are to be found in Canada, living among the Haudenosaunee on the Six Nations Reserve. Other Lenapes and Mahicans, who became known as the Stockbridge Munsee after living in Stockbridge, Massachussetts, were resettled in Wisconsin and live on the Stockbridge Munsee Reservation. Today more than 13,000 Lenape people are listed on tribal rolls recognized by the United States and Canada.

Mandan (Man'-dan)

The homeland of the Mandan, where they lived in about half a dozen villages made of permanent earth-lodges made of logs and clay, is near the present-day town of Mandan, close to Bismark, North Dakota. Each of their settlements was made up of twenty or more rectangular houses. Although they relied upon agriculture, they also hunted the buffalo each year when the seasonal migrations took the great herds past the Mandan villages. Along with their neighbors, the Hidatsa, who spoke a Siouan language similar to the Mandans', they were called the "farmers and merchants" of the northern plains, engaging in widespread trade with people as far away as the southwestern pueblos.

Known as skilled artisans and friends to such European explorers as Lewis and Clark, the Mandans suffered a terrible tragedy in 1837 when a smallpox epidemic hit. It is estimated that of the 1,600 Mandans only 31 survived. From that point on, the Mandans ceased to exist as a separate community. They joined with the surviving Hidatsa and Arikara and became known as the Three Affiliated Tribes. The Fort Berthold Reservation in North Dakota is the present-day home of the Mandan, Hidatsa and Arikara peoples. In 1954, with the filling of the Garrison Reservoir by the U.S. Army Corps of Engineers, the Three Affiliated Tribes lost over 150,000 acres from their reservation, including much of the best bottomland for farming.

Maya (My-uh)

More than five million Maya live today in their traditional homelands in eastern Mexico, Guatemala, Belize, Honduras and El Salvador. More than thirty Mayan languages are spoken, and Mayan history and stories were recorded for many centuries in writing on stone markers called *steles* and in pictographic books. The Mayan peoples are also known for their knowledge of mathematics and for their extremely accurate calendars, which are used to regulate both their ceremonies and their cycles of planting. The sophisticated civilization of the Mayan people is often associated with their "lost cities," such cities as Palenque and Chichen Itza, whose huge pyramids and other buildings made of stone have been uncovered in recent years in the dense jungles of Yucatan. However, the "Classic Period" of Mayan history, from about 250

A.D. to 900 A.D. represents only a part of the enduring lifestyle of the Mayan people. For more than 4,000 years they have planted their cornfields in forest gardens called *milpas*, using a style of agriculture which is much better suited to the forest ecosystem than "modern" methods.

The Lacandon Maya of Chiapas Province in Mexico are the most traditional and isolated of the Maya people, occupying a highland rainforest reserve which has shrunk in recent years to less than 2,200 square miles. The Lacandon community itself is concentrated in their small village of Naha, which numbers about 600 people. Their traditional stories often focus on the importance of human respect for the forest and their prophecies predict the end of all life on earth if the forests are destroyed.

O'odham (Ōh-ōh'-dum)

Known more commonly as the Papago, a name which means, literally, "The Bean People," a reflection of the practices of these people wise in the ways of the desert, the O'odham have long relied upon the plants of the desert—such as mesquite, which bears nutritious beans—for their food. Along with their cousins, the Pima, they call themselves O'odham, which means "The People." In addition to gathering a surprisingly wide variety of foods from the desert plants, they also made use of irrigation to grow cotton, corn and beans. Their dome-shaped lodges, perhaps 15 feet in diameter and made of a frame of saplings and thatched with leaves, blended seamlessly into the landscape.

More than 17,000 O'odham people remain in their homeland in the Sonoran Desert in the area near what is now Tucson, Arizona, and there is also a sizable population in Sonora, Mexico. They are well known today among art collectors for their complex and beautiful basketry, and agronomists have only recently begun to listen carefully to what these traditional people still have to tell them about the best ways to sustain agriculture in the desert.

Osage (Ōh'sāj)

"Osage" is a corruption of Wazhazhe, an Osage word meaning "true people." Their homelands are the eastern edge of the American plains in the tall-grass prairies of the area now known as eastern Kansas and western Missouri. Until the horse came, they did some hunting of the buffalo, but relied more heavily on agriculture, making use of the fertile lands along the rivers to grow their corn.

The Osage, even though they generally stood well over six feet (early French visitors to the Osage people met some Osage men who were seven feet tall!) called themselves "the little ones" to show their humility to Honga, "the Sacred One," Mother Earth. They regarded the animals around them as relatives and teachers and they passed down their traditions—which often were about the animals and the other wise beings of the natural world—in long prose poems which they called the *wi-gi-es*. The story of how the spider symbol came to them is found in one of those long epic traditions.

Relatives of the Omaha, Ponca and Quapaw, the Osage people were resettled by the U.S. government in Indian Territory. There are over 6,000 registered members of the Osage tribe today and their tribal offices are located in Pawhuska, Oklahoma.

Papago (Pah'-pah-gō)

See *O'odham*.

Passamaquoddy (Pass-uh-mah-kwah'-dee)

The name Passamaquoddy comes from the word *Peske-demakddi*, which means "plenty of pollock," a description of the seashore fishing area where these people live. The Passamaquoddy people, like the Penobscot, are among those Native nations called the Wabanaki, "the People of Land of the Dawn." Along with the Mic-macs, the Maliseet and the Abenakis of Quebec and western New England, they have been loosely allied since the early 1700s as the Wabanaki Confederacy, sharing similar languages and cultures. The home of the Passamaquoddy is the area along the eastern coast of Maine from Passamaquoddy Bay to present-day New Brunswick, Canada. More than 1,500 Passamaquoddy people today live on two reservations near Princeton and Perry, Maine. Although farming was important to the Passamaquoddy, their location near the ocean made fishing and food-gathering from the sea even more significant.

Unrecognized by the federal government for many years, the Passamaquoddy and the other Wabanaki nations of Maine maintained that their land had been taken illegally from them in the eighteenth and nineteenth centuries. In 1980, after years in the courts, President Carter signed the landmark Maine Indian Claims Settlement Act, which authorized $81.5 million to secure a land and financial base for the Passamaquoddy, Penobscot and Houlton Band of Maliseet in Maine and recognized the three tribes. In return, the tribes relinquished their claim to more than 12 million acres of land.

Passamaquoddy Ceremonial Days, generally held on August 1 feature pageantry, canoe races, social dances and singing. Strong efforts to preserve their culture and language have been underway for the last two decades. Recently, collections of stories and legends written in Passamaquoddy have been published by their bilingual education program.

Penobscot (Pen-ahb'-skaht)

The name Penobscot is derived from either *Pannawanbskek*, "it forks on the white rocks," *Penaubsket*, "it flows on rocks" or *Penobskat*, "plenty stones." Each of those is a good description of one part of their traditional homeland at the mouth of the Penobscot River near Castine, Maine. Like the Passamaquoddy, the Penobscot are in the Algonquian language family and made good use of the natural resources of both the seacoast and the inland areas, hunting, fishing, gathering and gardening in a seasonal round. The stories of their culture hero Gluskabe (called Koluskap among the Passamaquoddy) often contain pointed lessons in keeping the natural balance—what is today called environmentalism.

The Penobscot have a long history of friendship with the United States, dating back to the American Revolution when many of the Maine Indians supported the American side. They secured federal recognition in 1980 with the settlement of their land claims, which attempted to redress some of the wrong done to them in the previous two centuries. With the Passamaquoddy, they send a delegate to the Maine legislature. Their present-day reservation is located on the Penobscot River on Indian Island, one of a number of islands owned by their nation, and just over the bridge from Old Town, Maine. Today, Penobscot artisans are well known for their work in the areas of woodcarving and basket-making, and the arts and crafts stores on Indian Island offer examples of their artistry. More than 1,000 Penobscot are on their current tribal rolls.

Salish (Say'-lish)

The name Salish comes from the word "salst," and means "People." Salish is often used to refer to a family of related Native peoples, stretching from Montana through Idaho, northwest Washington and Southern British Columbia, who all share a similar language. Tribal nations referred to as "Salish" include the Okan-agan, the Colville, the Kalispel, the Spokane and numerous others. Salish is also the name given to a group of Native people whose traditional homeland is western Montana and who have been referred to in some cases as the "Flatheads." This is the name which was used by some of the other Native nations, who would bind the heads of their infants to shape their skulls, to describe the Salish people who did not do anything to shape the heads of their children.

The Salish people of Montana relied primarily on hunting and the gathering of wild plants. Today, the Confederated Salish and Kootenai Tribal Council is located in Pablo, Montana.

Seneca (Sen'-eh-ka)

The name Seneca does not come from Greek but from Native words meaning "People of the Stone." The Senecas, as the western-most of the Iroquois League, were the "Keepers of the Western Door of the Longhouse." Although there are contemporary Seneca communities in Canada at the Six Nations Reserve and in Oklahoma, where the Seneca Cayuga Tribe is located in Miami, Oklahoma, Seneca communities also remain in their original homeland, with reservations at Tonawanda and Cattaraugus in western New York. The Seneca Iroquois Museum in Salamanca, New York, contains many interesting exhibits about Seneca culture and history. See also *Haudenosaunee*.

Snoqualmie (Snōw-kwal'-mē)

The name Snoqualmie means "People of the Moon," and comes from a traditional story which says that the Snoqualmie people originated from the Moon. A division of the Salish and relatives of the Duwamish and Suquamish, the people of the well-known Native leader Chief Seattle, the Snoqualmie peoples' traditional home is around present-day Seattle in the state of Washington. Like the other Native people of the region, gathering plants from the fields and forests, hunting game and salmon fishing were of more importance for their subsistence than agriculture. See also *Salish*.

Tuscarora (Tus-ka-rō'-rah)

The "Sixth Nation" of the Iroquois, the Tuscarora or "Shirt-wearing People" originally lived in the area of North Carolina before being dispossessed in the eighteenth century. Today, the Tus-carora Reservation is located in western New York, not far from Niagara Falls, where the Turtle Museum is run by the Tuscarora people. See also *Haudenosaunee*.

Wampanoag (Wom-pah-nō'-ag)

The past and present homeland of the Wampanoag, whose name means "Land of First Light," is the Massachussetts Coast. It was the Wampanoag people who helped the Pilgrims to survive, teaching them how to grow corn, beans and squash, and how to hunt and fish and gather such things as clams from the shores. The clam-bake, now a part of New England life, was a Wampanoag tradition. Around 1621, the Wampanoags celebrated the "first" Thanksgiving with the Pilgrims. Such ceremonies of giving thanks for various harvests, however, had been a part of the Wampanoag way of life since time immemorial.

Despite Puritan intolerence for their way of life and the continued taking of Native land, Massasoit, the chief of the Wampanoag, pursued a policy of peace throughout his lifetime, sending his sons Metacomet and Wamsutta to the Puritan schools. It was not until the Wampanoags under Metacomet (also known as King Philip) became the first to form a Native confederacy, that an organized attempt was made to drive the English from their land. That two-year armed conflict, which saw the destruction of many English settlements, became known as King Philip's War and was narrowly won by the English. Following that war many of the Wampanoag were sold as slaves to the West Indies or made indentured servants.

Despite their losses, the Wampanoags survived in their two major communities in Massachussets of Gay Head on the island of Martha's Vineyard and Mashpee on Cape Cod. However, their continued existence—like that of numerous other tribal nations in the eastern part of the United States—was ignored or denied by the government. During the 1920s the Wampanoag people began to work to reorganize and revitalize their nation. In 1987, the Gay Head Wampanoag won federal recognition as an Indian tribe.

Other Versions of Native North American Stories

In choosing the stories to be included in this book and in its two predecessors, I followed several rules. First, I chose stories with levels of meaning a general audience can understand. (Each story has additional levels of meaning to be perceived by those who are close to the individual tribal nation each story comes from.) Second, I did not tell "restricted" stories, stories only to be shared with those who are, in some way, "initiated." Third, I only included stories with earlier versions already in print or in public circulation through recordings or film. I do not wish to be the first to take a story out of the oral tradition. Fourth, the versions included in this book (and in *Native American Stories* and *Native American Animal Stories)* are my own retellings and may differ from other versions already recorded. I have tried to make my versions closer to the oral traditions from which they came or to include important information left out in other recorded tellings.

My retellings of each of the stories have been based on assistance from other Native storytellers and writers and on my knowledge of other written versions of these tales. The following is an acknowledgment of those tellers and a suggestion of places to look for other written tellings of the stories.

The Corn Spirit (Seneca/Tuscarora). My thanks to Marion Miller, Seneca storyteller. There are many other versions of the corn spirit story. In some cases the corn spirit is a woman, in others, a man. See Arthur Parker's *Seneca Myths and Folk Tales* (University of Nebraska Press, 1989); *Seneca Fiction, Legends and Myths* by J. N. B. Hewitt (Washington, D.C.: Bureau of American Ethnology Report 32, 1911).

The Sky Tree (Huron). Thanks to my Huron (Wyandot) friends Eleonore Jiconsaseh Sioui and George B. Sioui. See *The Huron* by Nancy Bonvillian (Chelsea House, 1989).

How Kishelemukong Made the People and the Seasons (Lenape). Special thanks to Jack Forbes (Lenape/Renape) for his work in preserving and explaining Lenape traditions. See *The Lenapes* by Robert S. Grumet (Chelsea House, 1989).

The Thanks to the Trees (Seneca). This section from the traditional Seneca Thanksgiving Address, which is given at the start of most important gatherings, is adapted and translated from a Long Opening Thanksgiving Address given in 1972 by Enos Williams/Quivering Leaves at Seneca Longhouse, Six Nations, Ontario. The full text of a Mohawk version entitled *Thanksgiving Address: Greetings to the Natural World*, illustrated by Kahionhes and edited by John Stokes, is available from The Tracking Project, PO Box 266, Corrales, NM 87048. It is not for sale, but contributions are accepted to keep the book in print. (I suggest offering at least $5.)

The Circle of Life and the Clambake (Wampanoag). Russell Peters is my primary source for this story. See *Wampanoag Tales: Legends of Maushop* (Story Stone), an audiocassette by Wampanoag storyteller Medicine Story and in *Spirit of the New England Tribes: Indian History & Folklore, 1620–1984* by William S. Simmons (University Press of New England, 1986).

Fallen Star's Ears (Cheyenne). Thanks to Lance Henson for keeping Cheyenne traditions and helping me understand them.

See *Star Legends Among the American Indians* by Clark Wissler, American Museum of Natural History Science Guide #91; *The Rolling Head* by Henry Tall Bull and Tom Weist (Montana Indian Publications).

Koluskap and Malsom (Passamaquoddy). Several versions of this story, which is much like the Iroquois tradition of the twin sons of Sky Woman's daughter, are told among the different Wabanaki nations, including my own Missisquoi Abenaki people. See *The Wabanakis of Maine and the Maritimes*, prepared and published for the Maine Indian Program by the American Friends Service Committee.

Why Some Trees Are Always Green (Cherokee). Gayl Ross and Murv Jacob are foremost among the Cherokee storytellers and artists who have helped me. See *The Path to Snowbird Mountain* by Traveller Bird (Farrar, Straus & Giroux, 1972); *Myths of the Cherokee* by James Mooney (Washington, D.C.: Bureau of American Ethnology Report 19, 1902).

The Bitterroot (Salish). Thanks to Vi Hilbert and Johnny Moses. See *Indian Legends from the Northern Rockies* by Ella E. Clark (University of Oklahoma Press, 1988).

Indian Summer (Penobscot). Penobscot storyteller Joe Mitchell of Old Town, Maine, is only one of a number of contemporary Abenaki storytellers. See "Penobscot Tales and Religious Beliefs" by Frank G. Speck, *Journal of American Folklore* No. 187.

The First Basket (Mandan). See *Prairie Smoke* by Melvin R. Gilmore (Minnesota Historical Society Press, 1987).

The Woman Who Lives in the Earth (Chugach Inuit). Mary Peters, an Inuit storyteller, was kind enough to spend several hours sharing stories with me when I visited her in 1992 on Baffin Island. Much of my understanding of her people and their stories comes from her and the other elders who were so generous to me. See *Powers Which We Do Not Know: The Gods and Spirits of the Inuit* by Daniel Merkur (University of Idaho, 1991).

Waw Giwulk: The Center of the Basket (O'odham). Thanks to Larry Evers. See "Pima and Papago Legends," by Mary L. Neff, *Journal of American Folklore* 25, 1912.

How Fox Brought the Forests from the Sky (Snoqualmie). See *Indian Legends of the Pacific Northwest* by Ella E. Clark (University of California Press, 1953).

The People of Maize (Maya). Thanks to Victor Montejo of the Jkaltek and Chan Kin, the 120-year-old patriarch of the Lacandon Mayan village of Naha, who shared many stories with me when I visited his people in 1992 in the Mexican rainforest. The best-known written version of this tale can be found in *Popol Vuh: The Sacred Book of the Ancient Quiche Maya* by Adrian Recinos as translated by Goetz and Morley (University of Oklahoma Press, 1983).

Waynabozho and the Wild Rice (Anishinabe). See *Wild Rice and the Ojibwa People* by Thomas Vennum, Jr. (Minnesota Historical Society Press, 1988).

The Buffalo Bull and the Cedar Tree (Osage). See *Osage Life and Legends* by Robert Liebert (Happy Camp, Calif.: Naturegraph, 1987); *The Osage Tribe* by Francis LaFlesche (Washington, D.C.: Bureau of American Ethnology Report 35, 1918).

The Keepers Series

by Michael J. Caduto and Joseph Bruchac

The books and tapes in the highly acclaimed Keepers Series have become North American environmental classics and bestsellers.

Keepers of the Earth: Native Stories and Environmental Activities for Children is a wonderful resource for teachers, parents, naturalists, and outdoor educators. A synthesis of the wisdom found in traditional Native stories with hands-on learning activities for children ages 5 to 12 teach environmental understanding and stewardship. 240 pages • 8½" x 11" hardcover • ISBN 0-920079-57-1

The Teacher's Guide to Keepers of the Earth expands upon the educational philosophy behind linking Native stories with environmental activities, and places the traditional stories in the context of their Native cultures. 48 pages • 8½" x 11" paperback • ISBN 0-920079-97-0

The Native Stories from Keepers of the Earth are superbly told and illustrated stories from a variety of aboriginal groups of North America — including Inuit, Micmac, Mohawk, Zuni, Hopi, and many others — that show we are entrusted with the responsibility to maintain the natural balance, to take care of our mother, to be keepers of the Earth. For readers of all ages.
160 pages • 7" x 10" paperback • ISBN 0-920079-76-8

Keepers of the Earth Audiocassettes contain the complete, unabridged stories from *Keepers of the Earth*, told by Native storyteller Joseph Bruchac and accompanied by Native music.
2 audiocassettes • approx. 133 minutes • ISBN 1-55591-099-8

Keepers of the Animals: Native Stories and Wildlife Activities for Children continues the tradition, this time with stories that demonstrate the importance of animals in Native traditions and promote a wildlife conservation ethic. The book provides a complete program of study in wildlife ecology and environmental issues concerning animals. 268 pages • 8½" x 11" hardcover • ISBN 0-920079-88-1

The Teacher's Guide to Keepers of the Animals, the companion volume to *Keepers of the Animals*, provides background information on storytelling and on the Native North American cultures that created the stories. 48 pages • 8½" x 11" paperback • ISBN 1-55591-107-2

The Native Stories from Keepers of the Animals are traditional Native stories that hold the power and wisdom to help us learn to live in balance with other life on Earth. Parents, teachers, and children will cherish these lovingly told tales about "our relations, the animals."
160 pages • 7" x 10" paperback • ISBN 1-895618-19-3

Keepers of the Animals Audiocassettes contain the complete, unabridged stories from *Keepers of the Animals*, told by author Joseph Bruchac and accompanied by Native music.
2 audiocassettes • approx. 107 minutes • ISBN 1-55591-128-5

Keepers of the Night: Native Stories and Nocturnal Activities for Children offers a comprehensive study of important topics in astronomy, night time weather, and nocturnal plants and animals from habitats throughout North America. Through traditional Native stories, information, and activities, the world of the night comes vibrantly to life. 160 pages • 7" x 10" paperback • ISBN 1-895618-39-8

Keepers of Life: Discovering Plants Through Native Stories and Earth Activities for Children, from which the stories in this collection were taken, provides a complete program of study in botany, plant ecology, and the natural history of plants from all North American habitats.
260 pages • 8½" x 11" hardcover • ISBN 1-895618-48-7